Mandalas, with their intricate shapes and delicate patterns, have the power to transport us to a state of deep serenity.

They are portals to a peaceful mind, offering a welcoming refuge from the challenges of everyday life.

This book is more than simply a collection of coloring pages; It is an invitation to explore your inner world, find balance and discover joy in the simplicity of each stroke.

Each floral mandala has been carefully selected to provide not only a visually rewarding experience, but also an opportunity for introspection and relaxation.

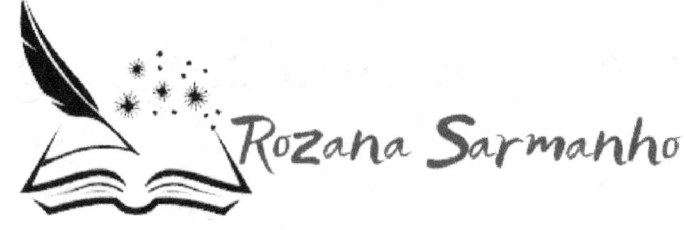

Test Color Page

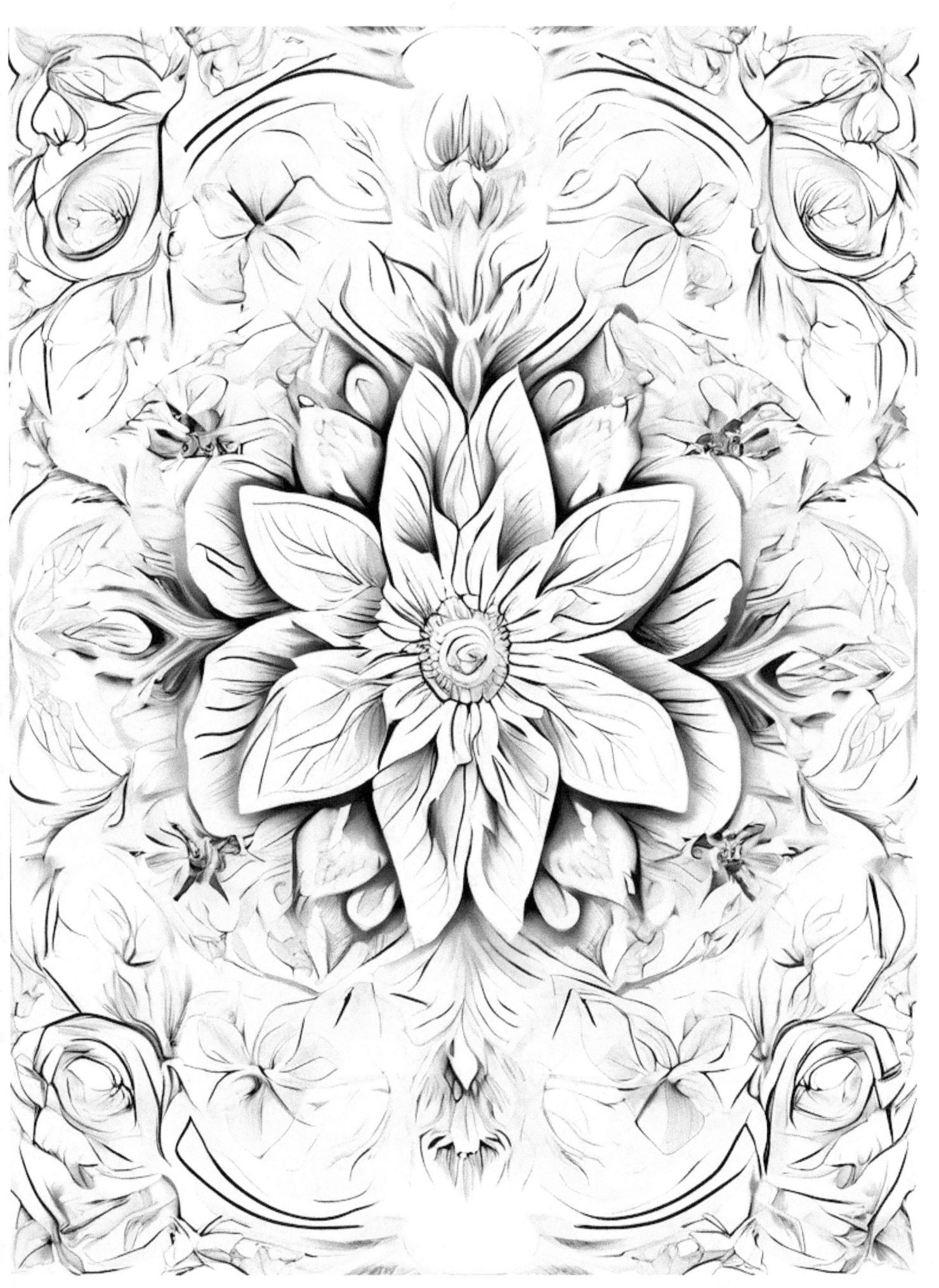

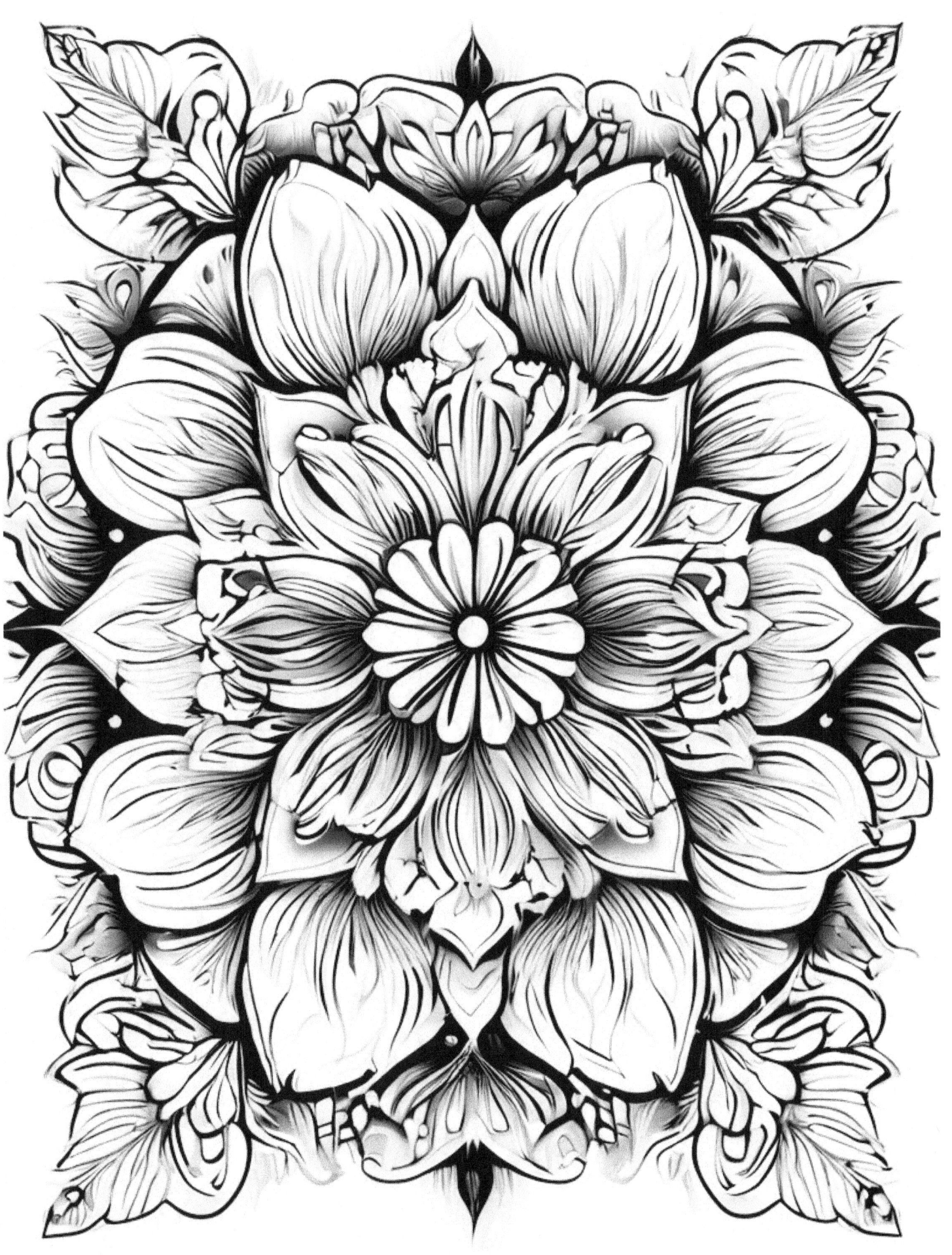

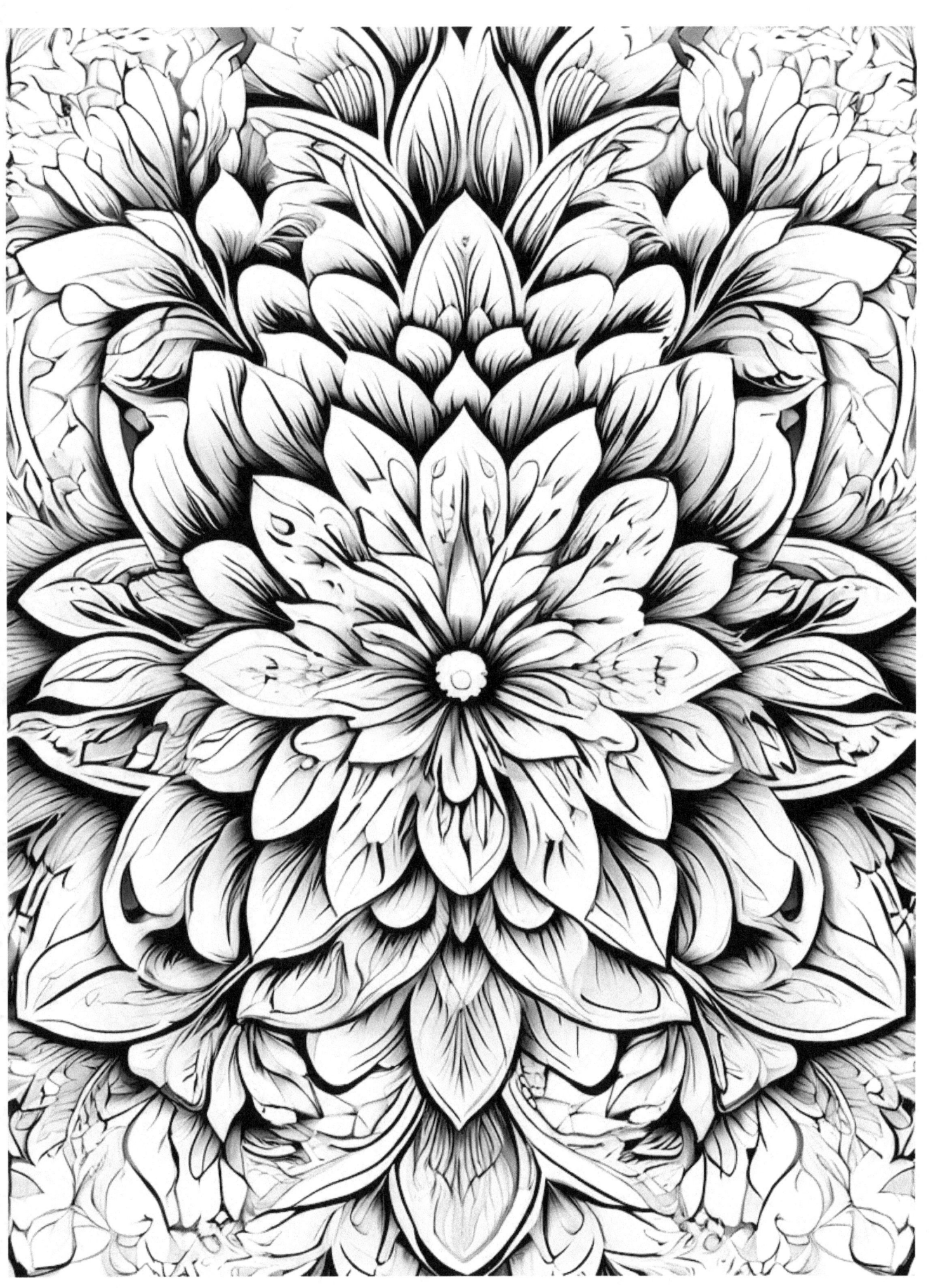

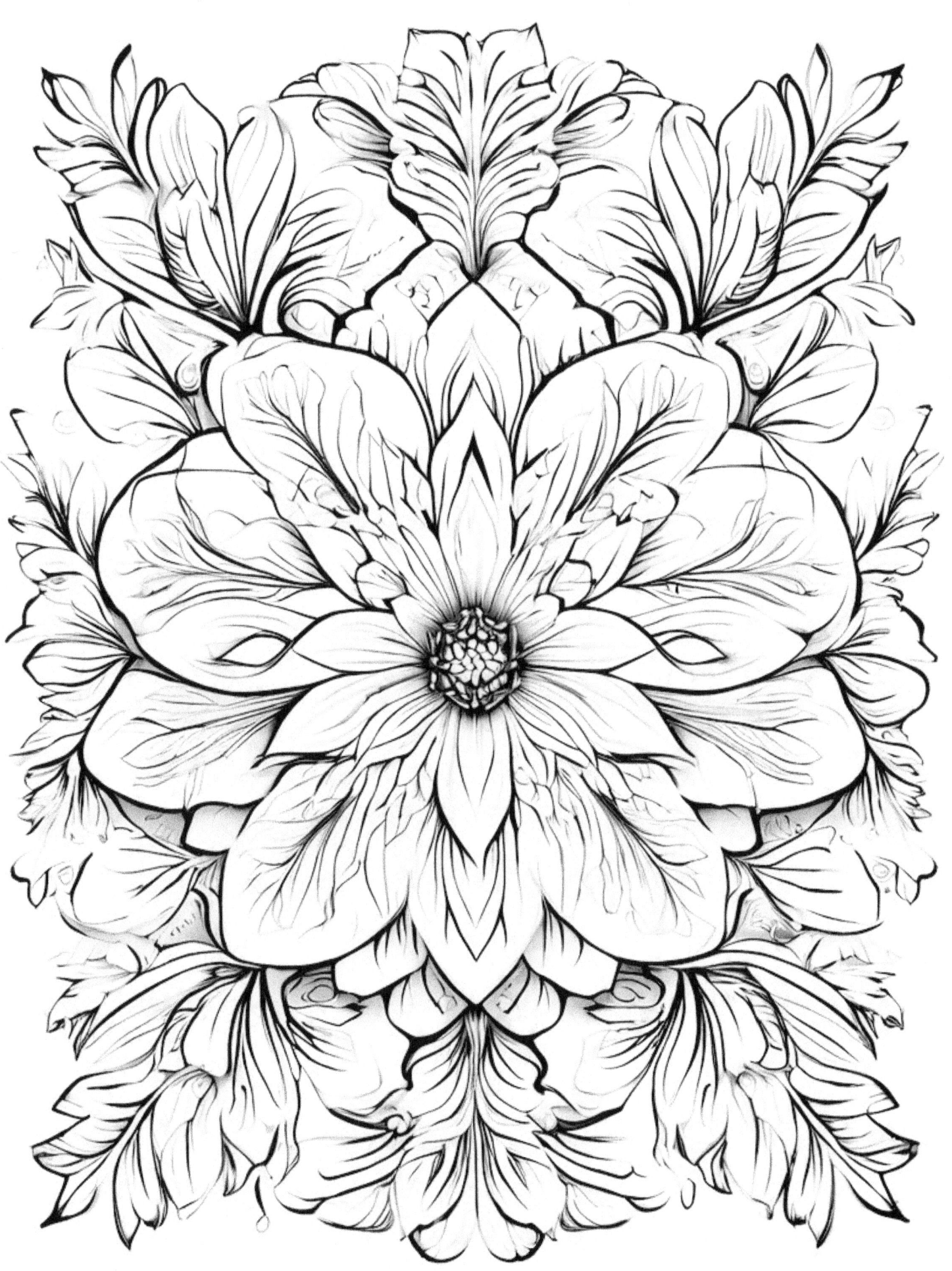

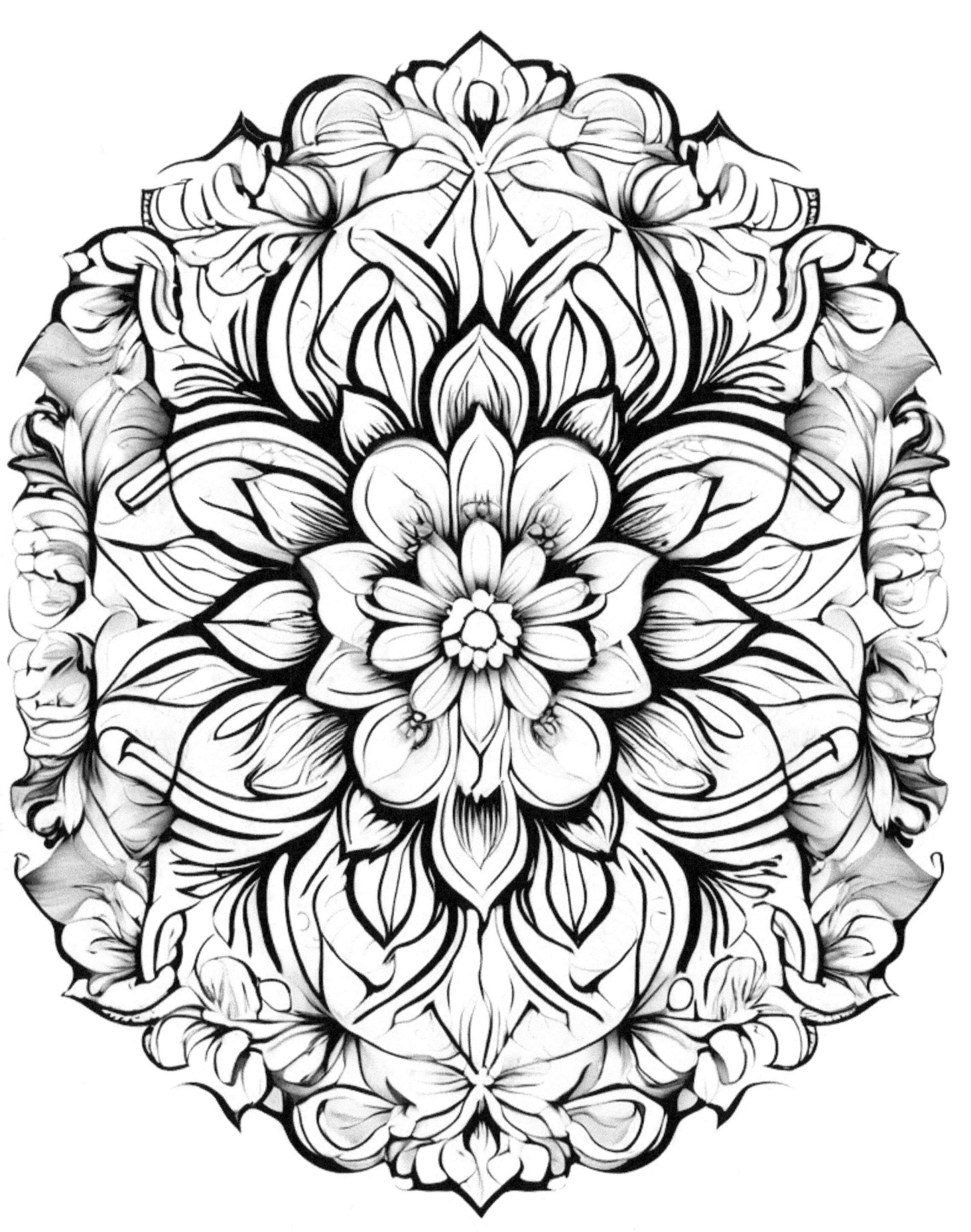

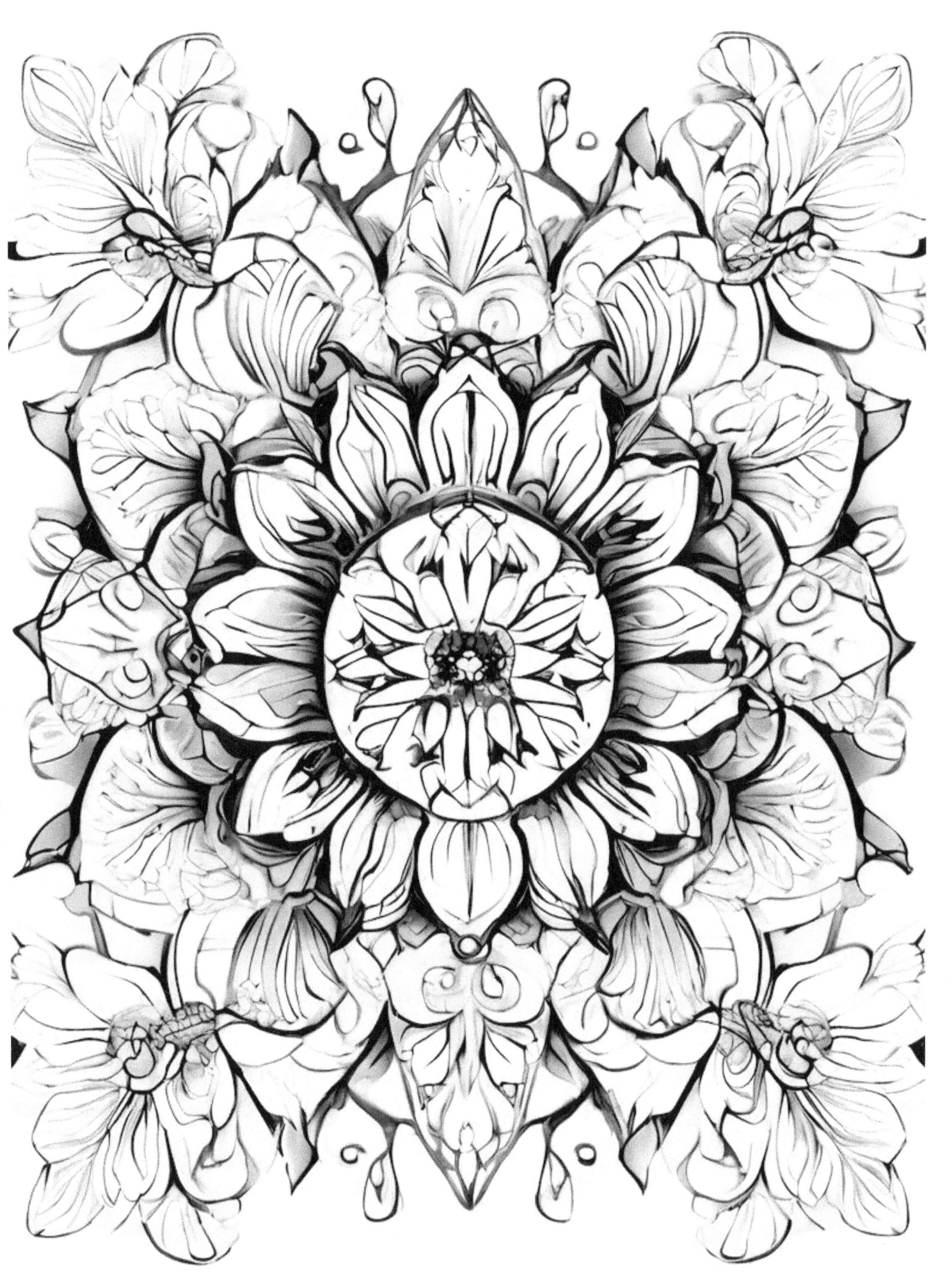

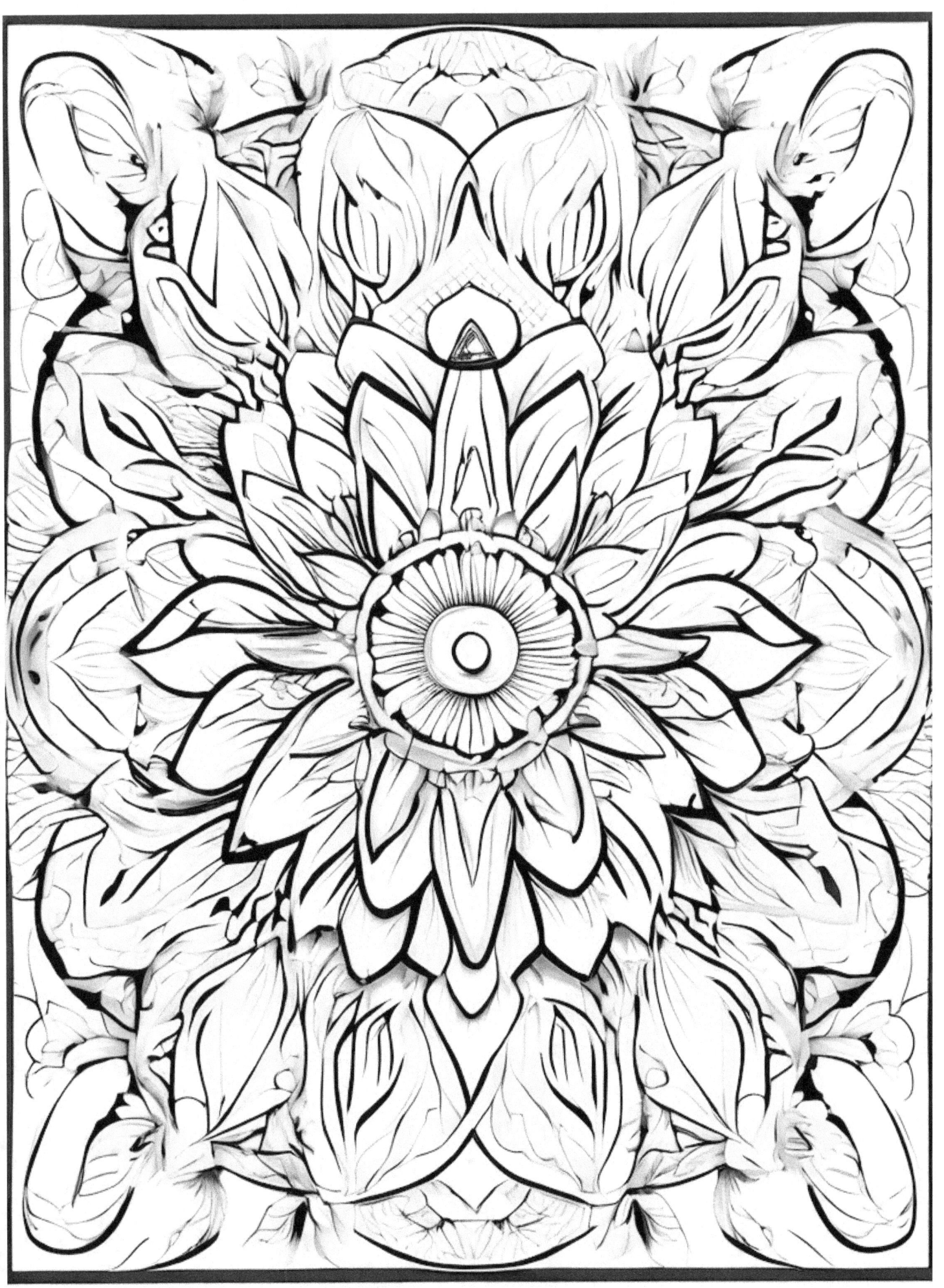

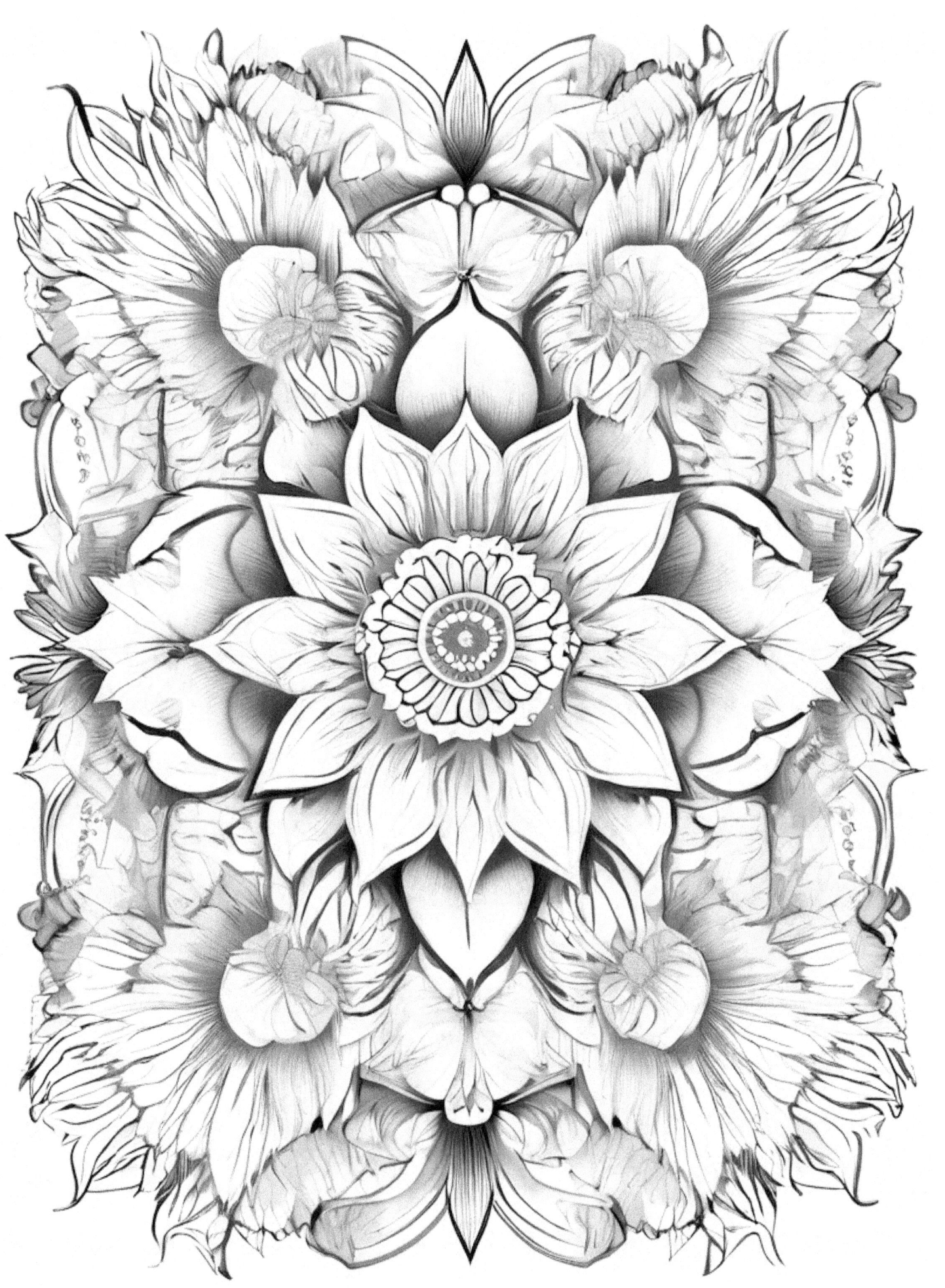

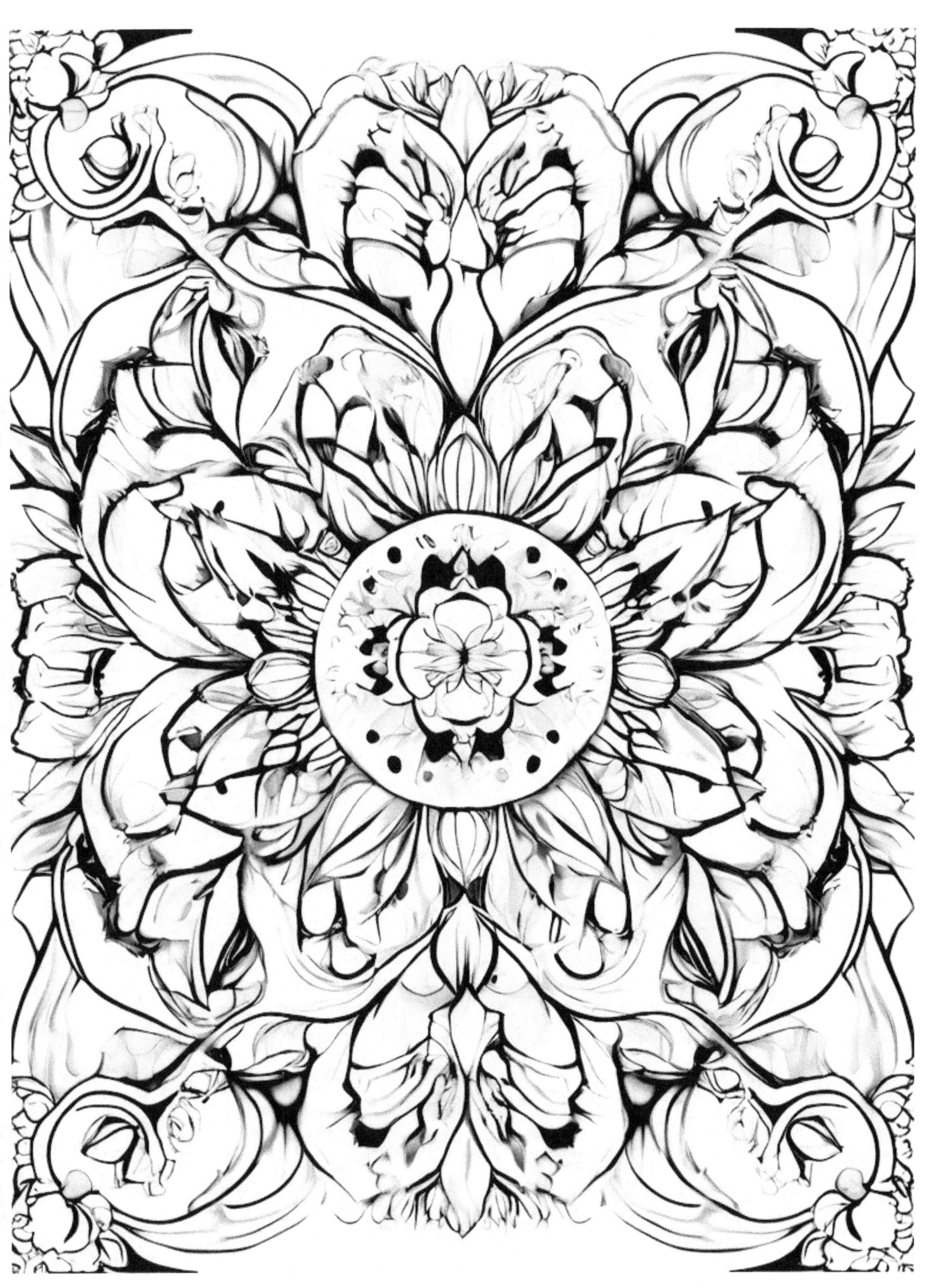

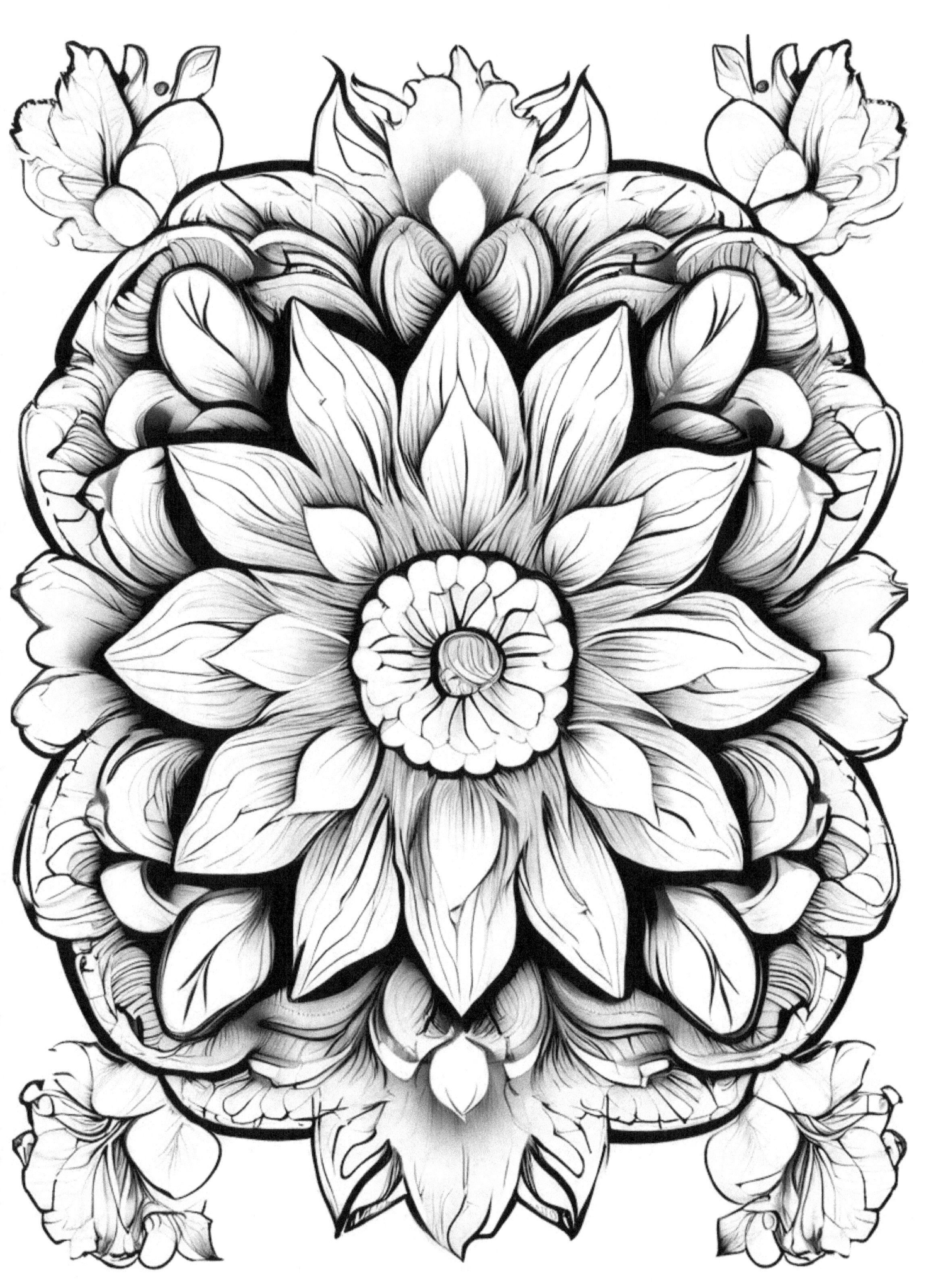

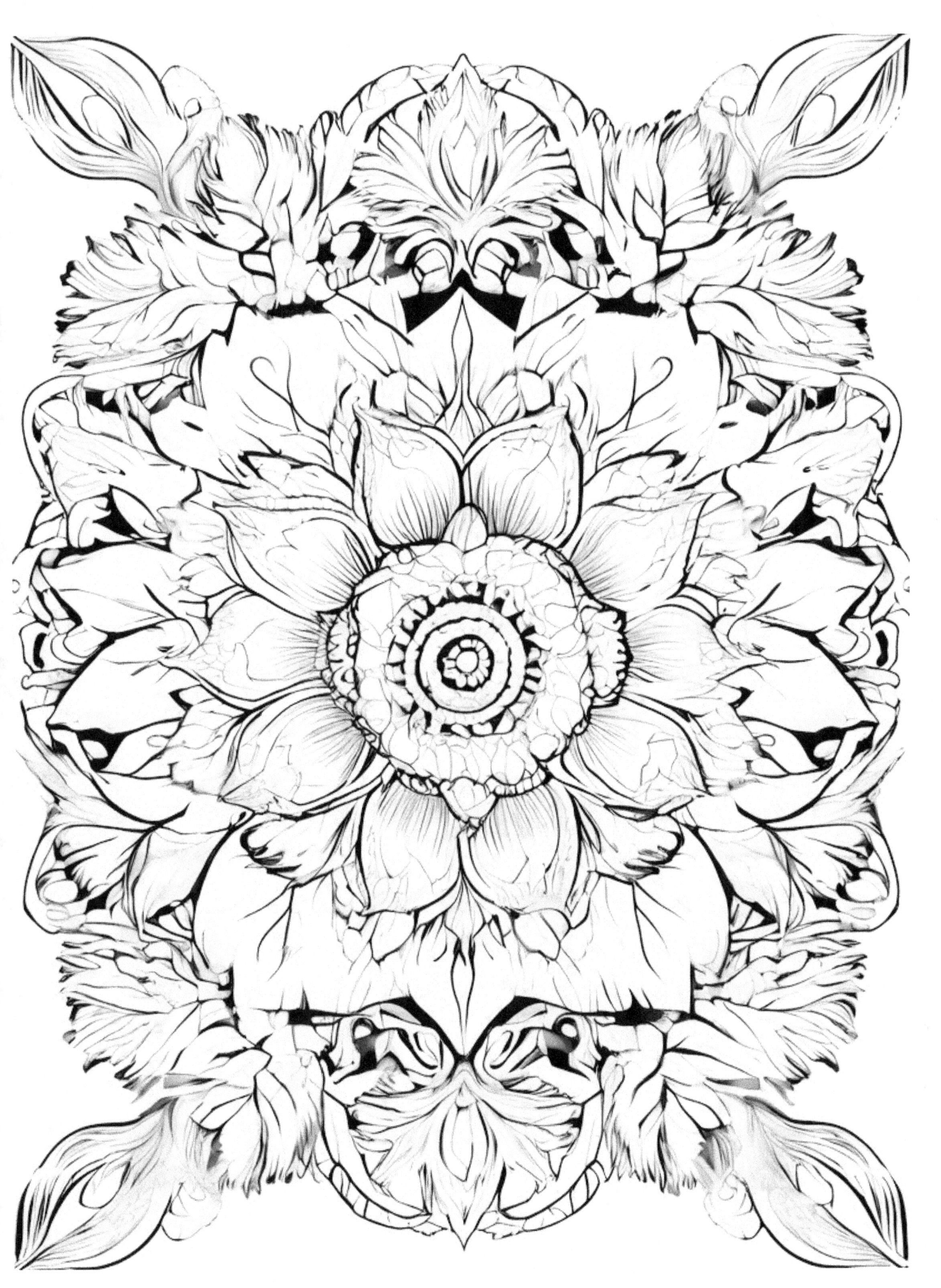

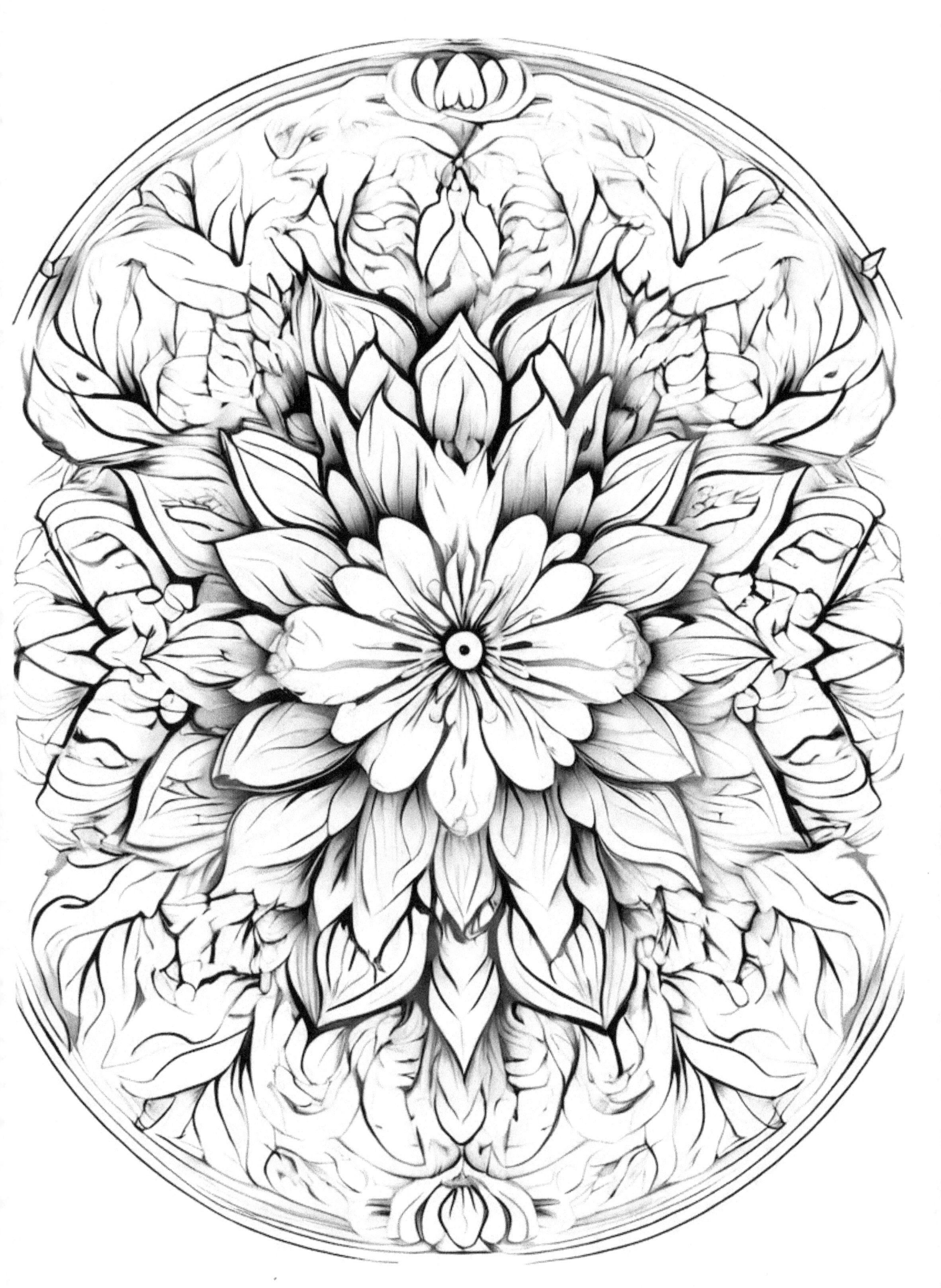

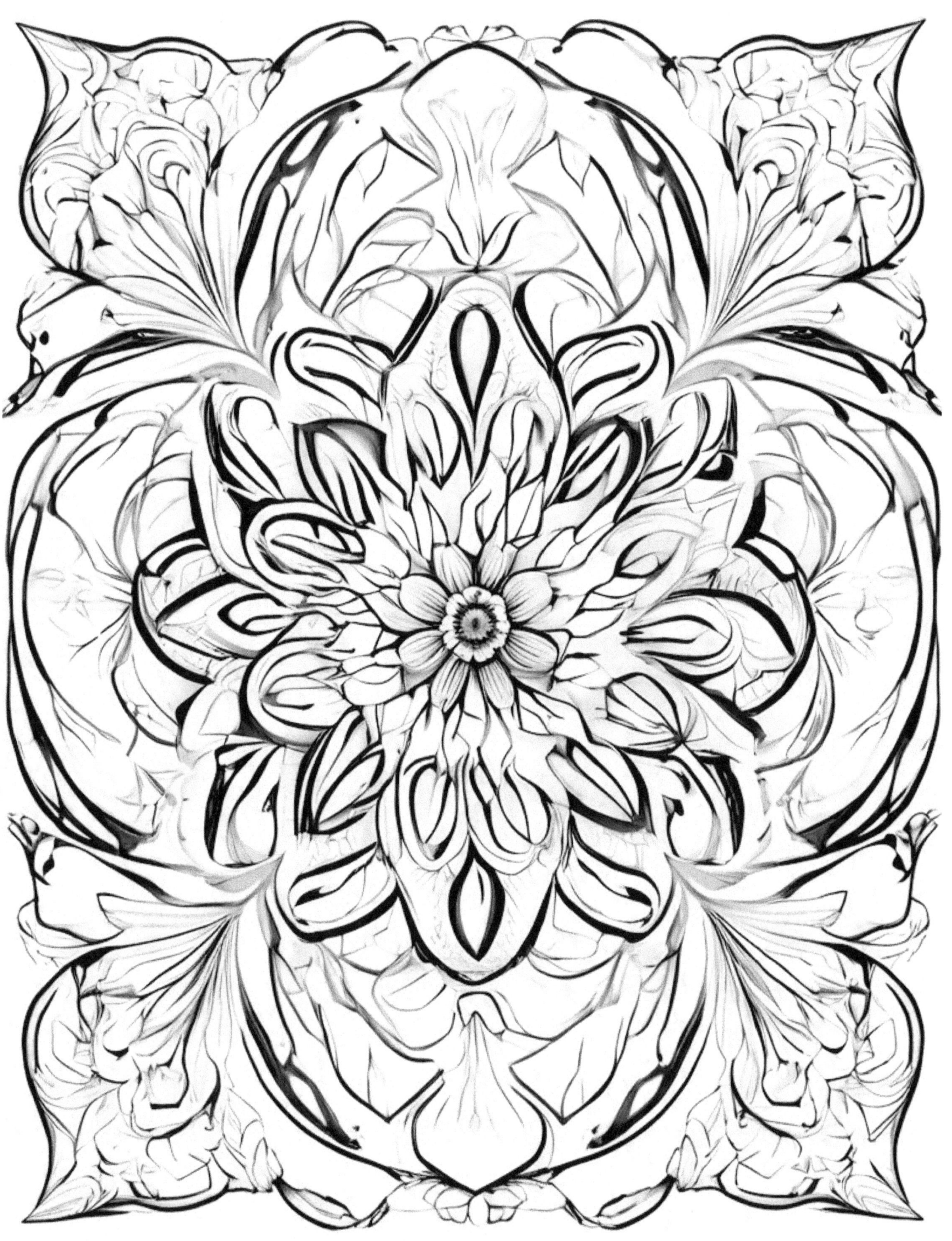

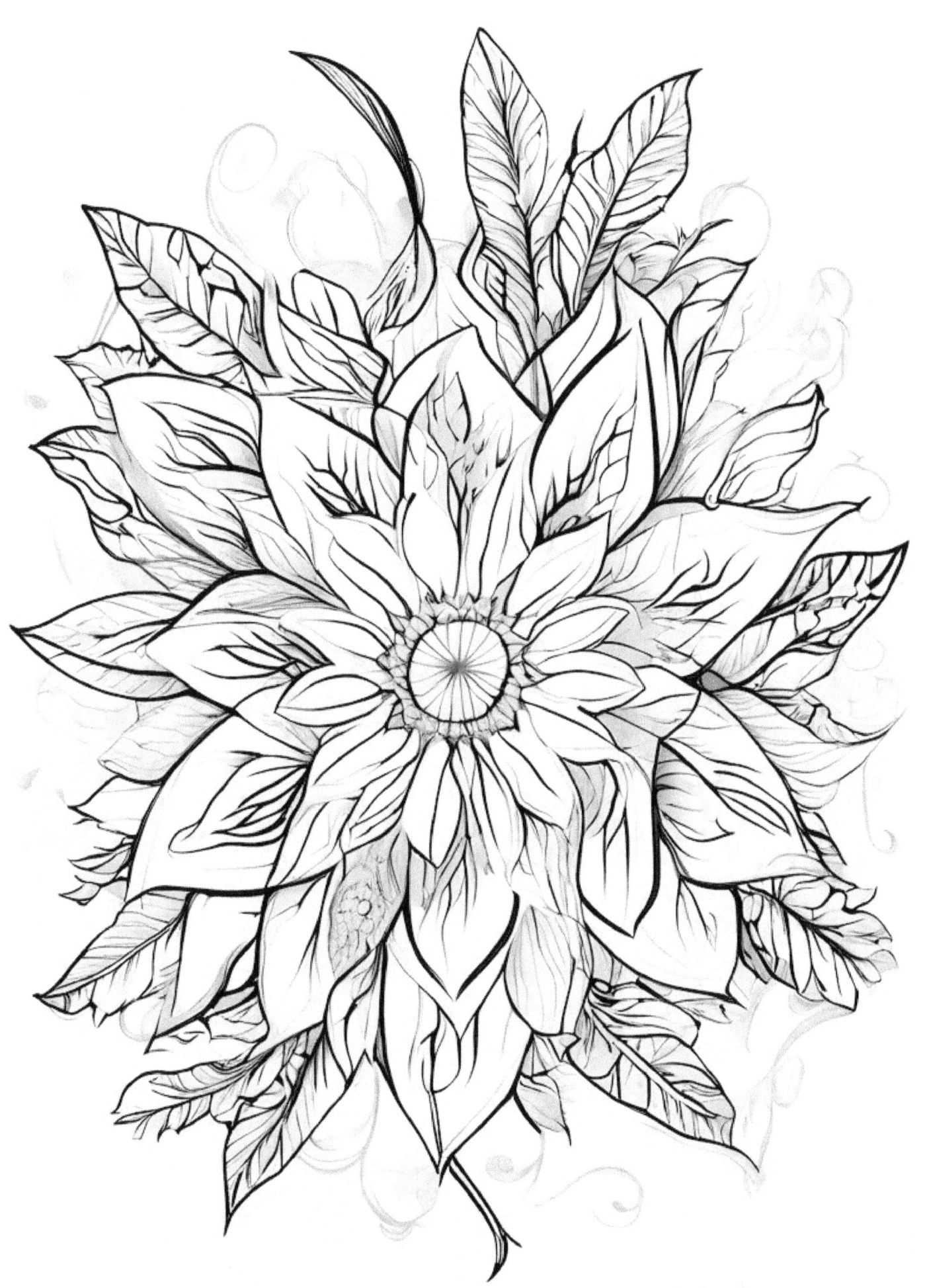

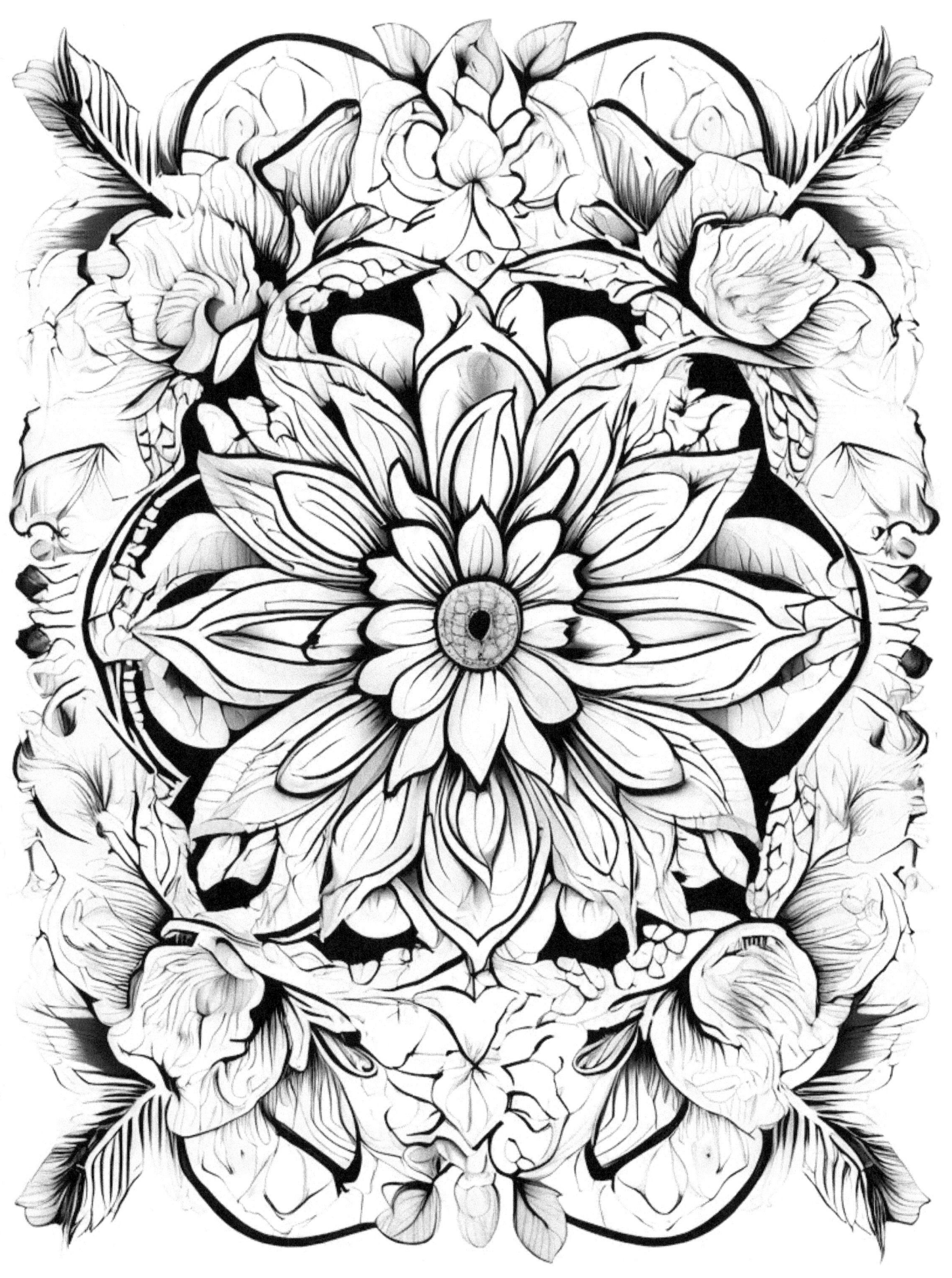

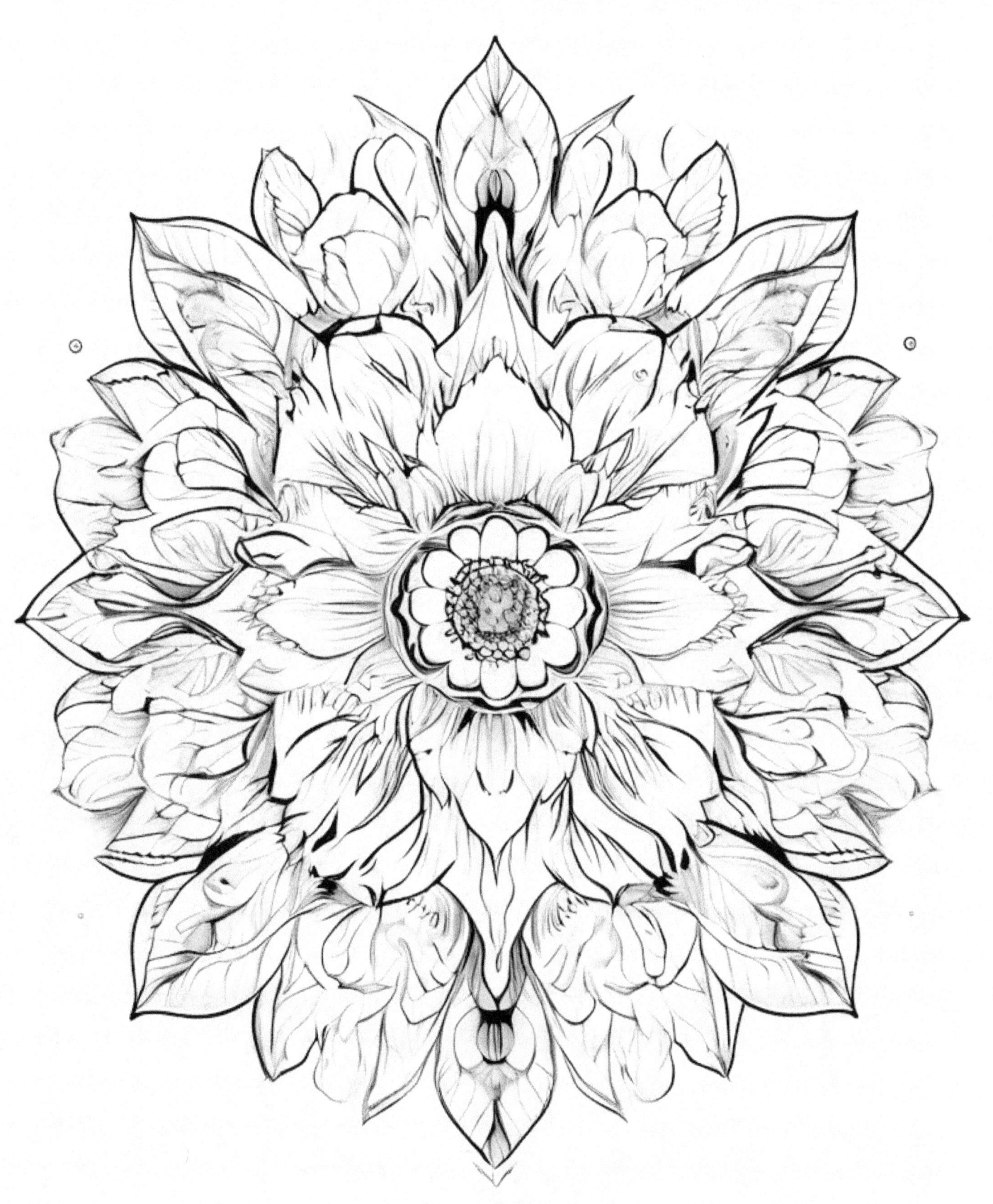

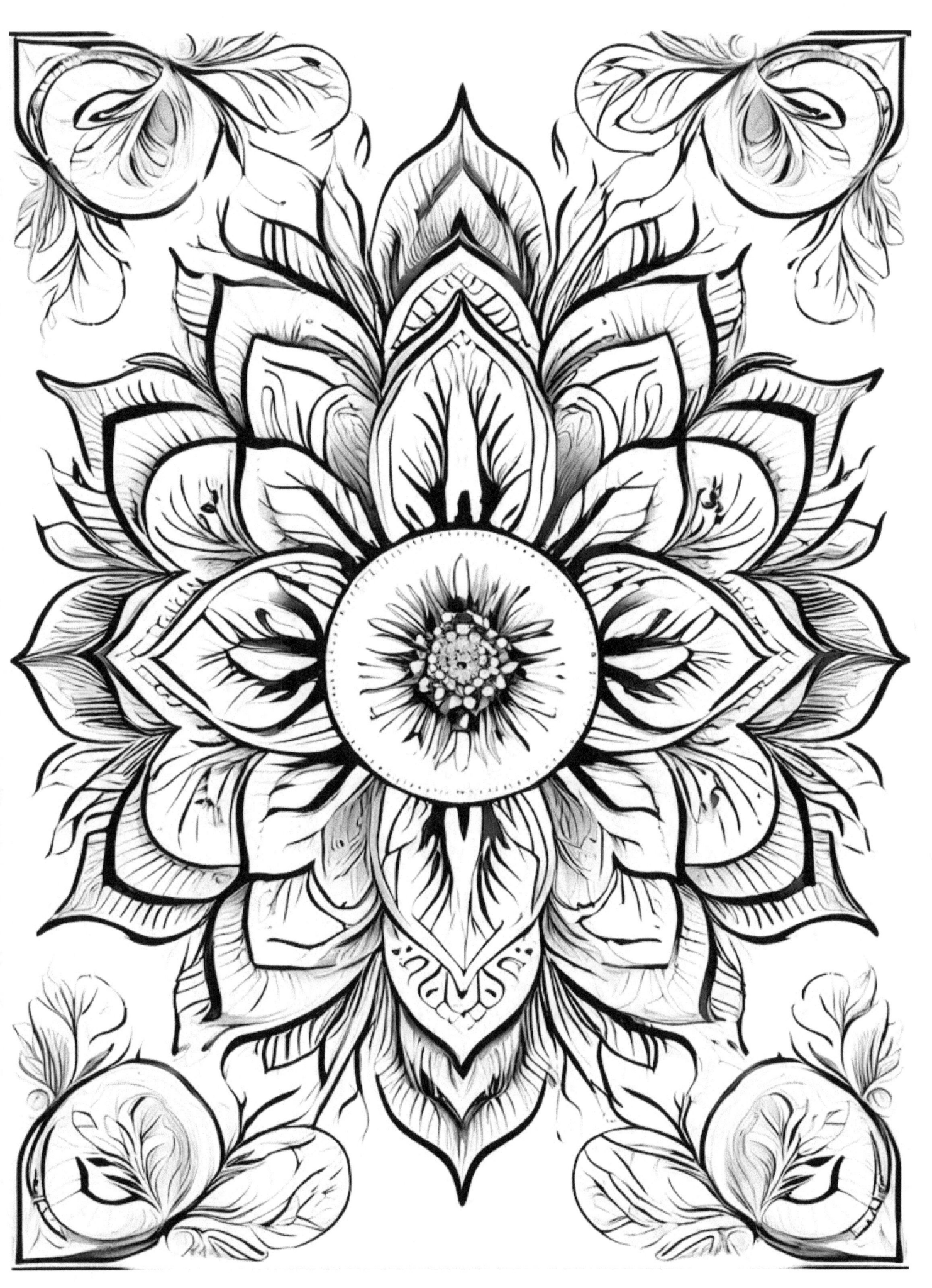

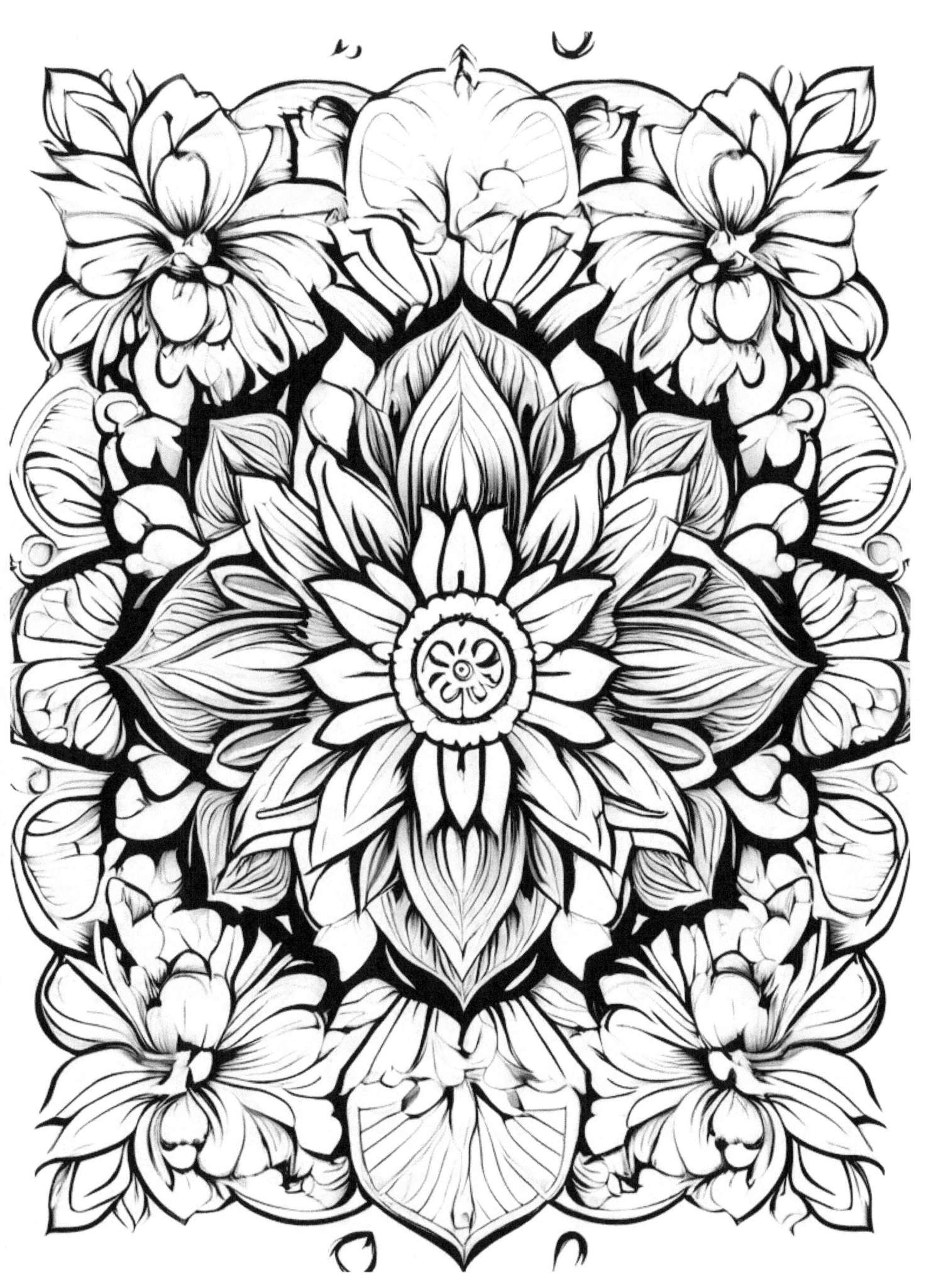

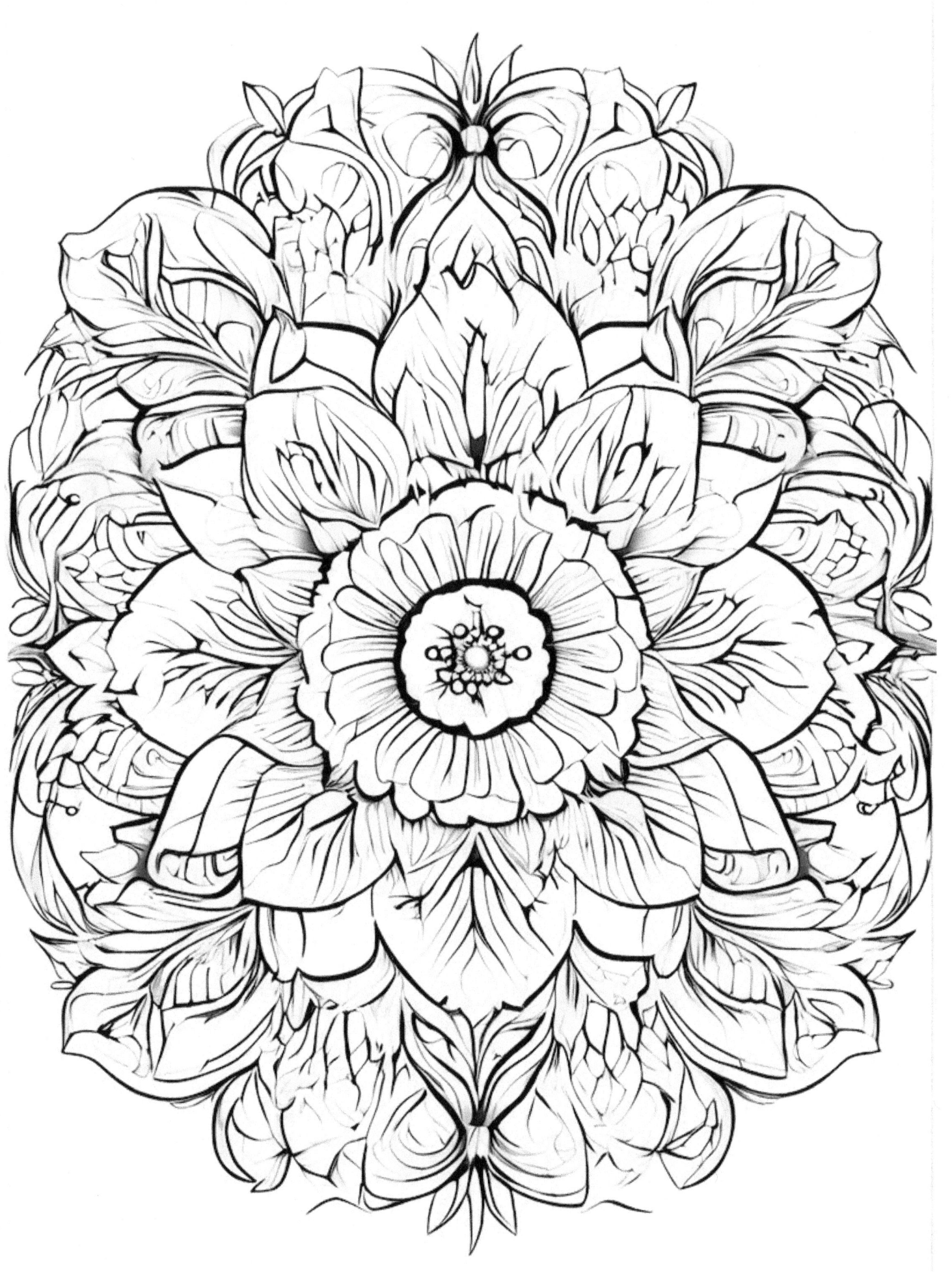

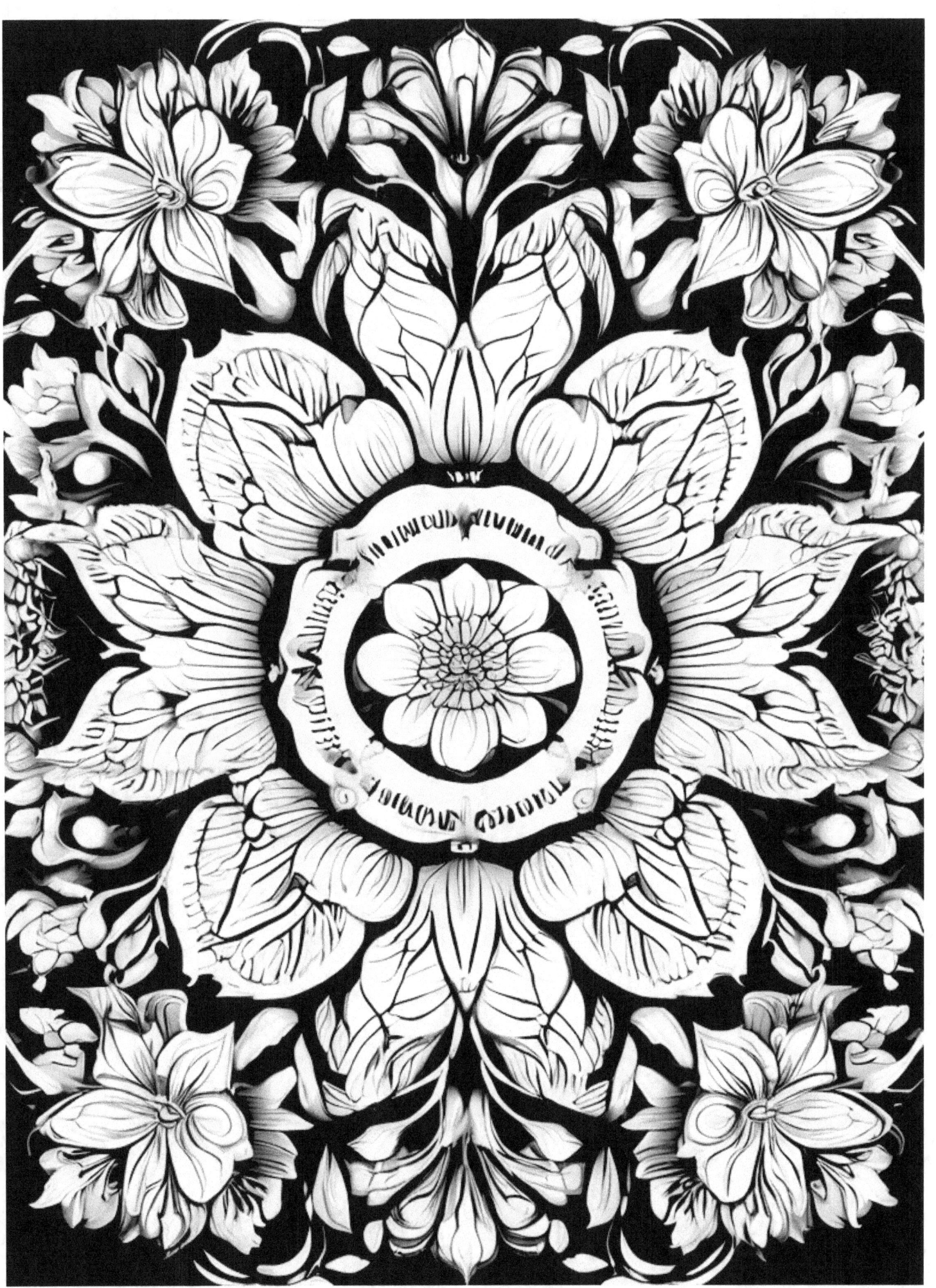

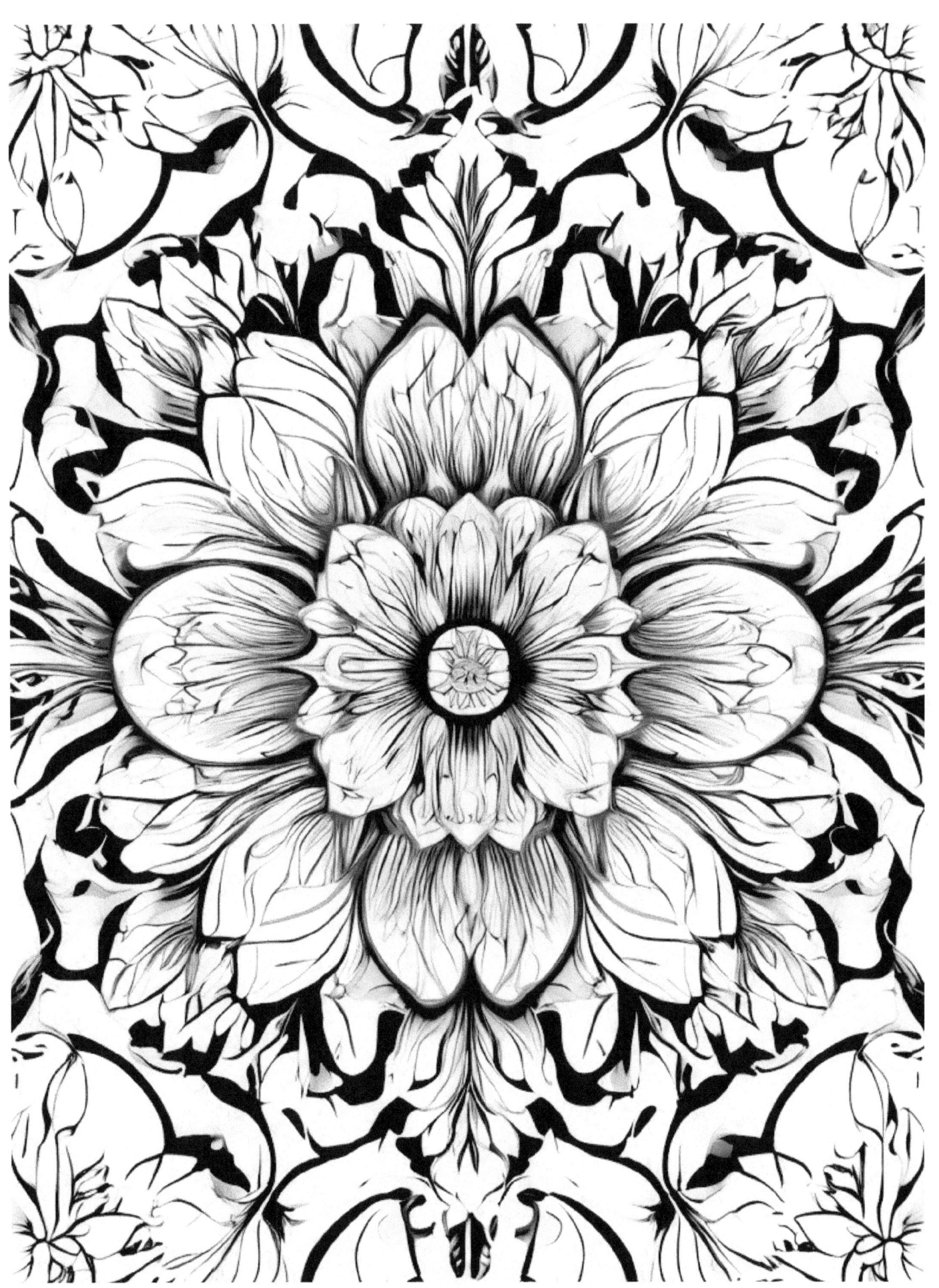

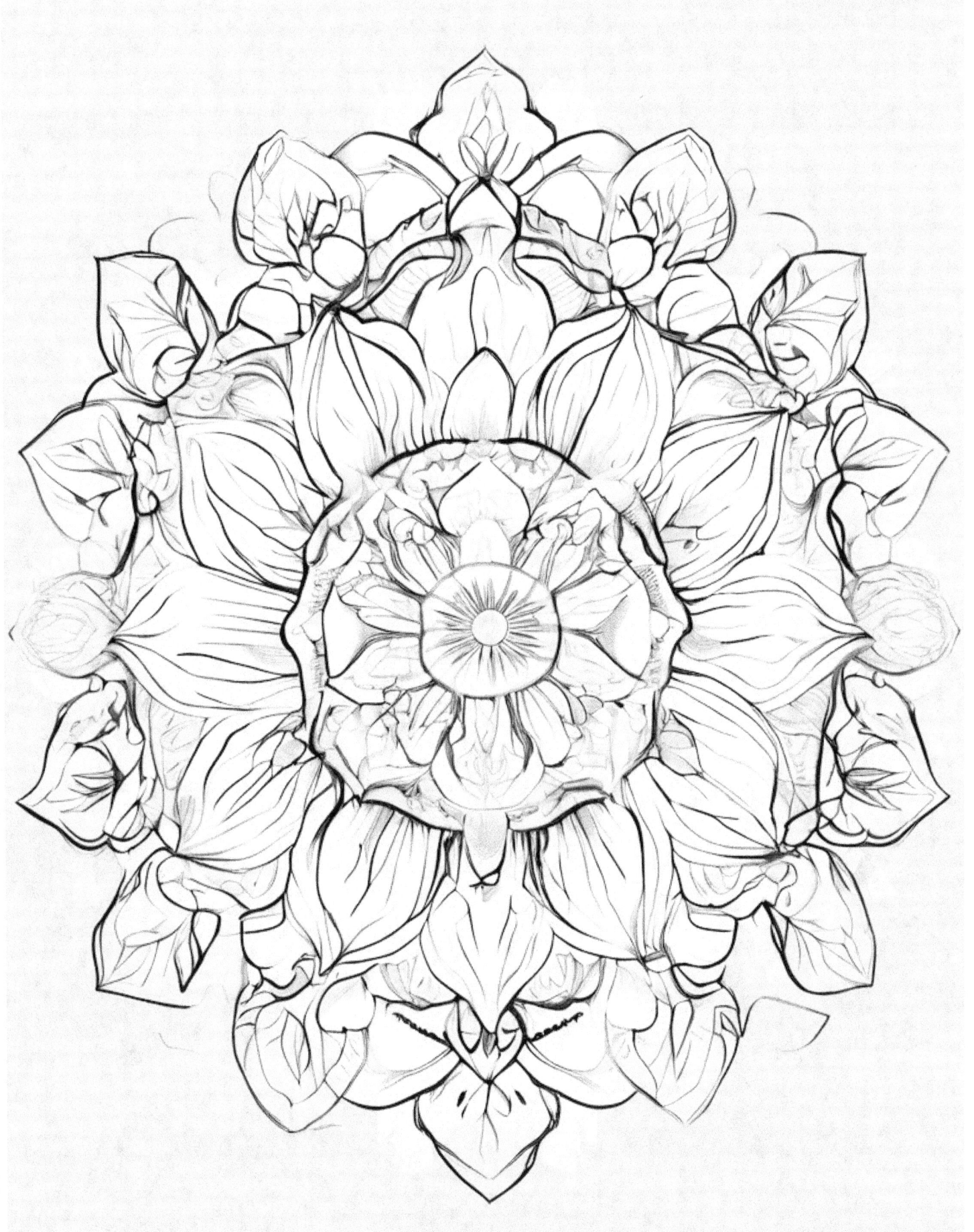

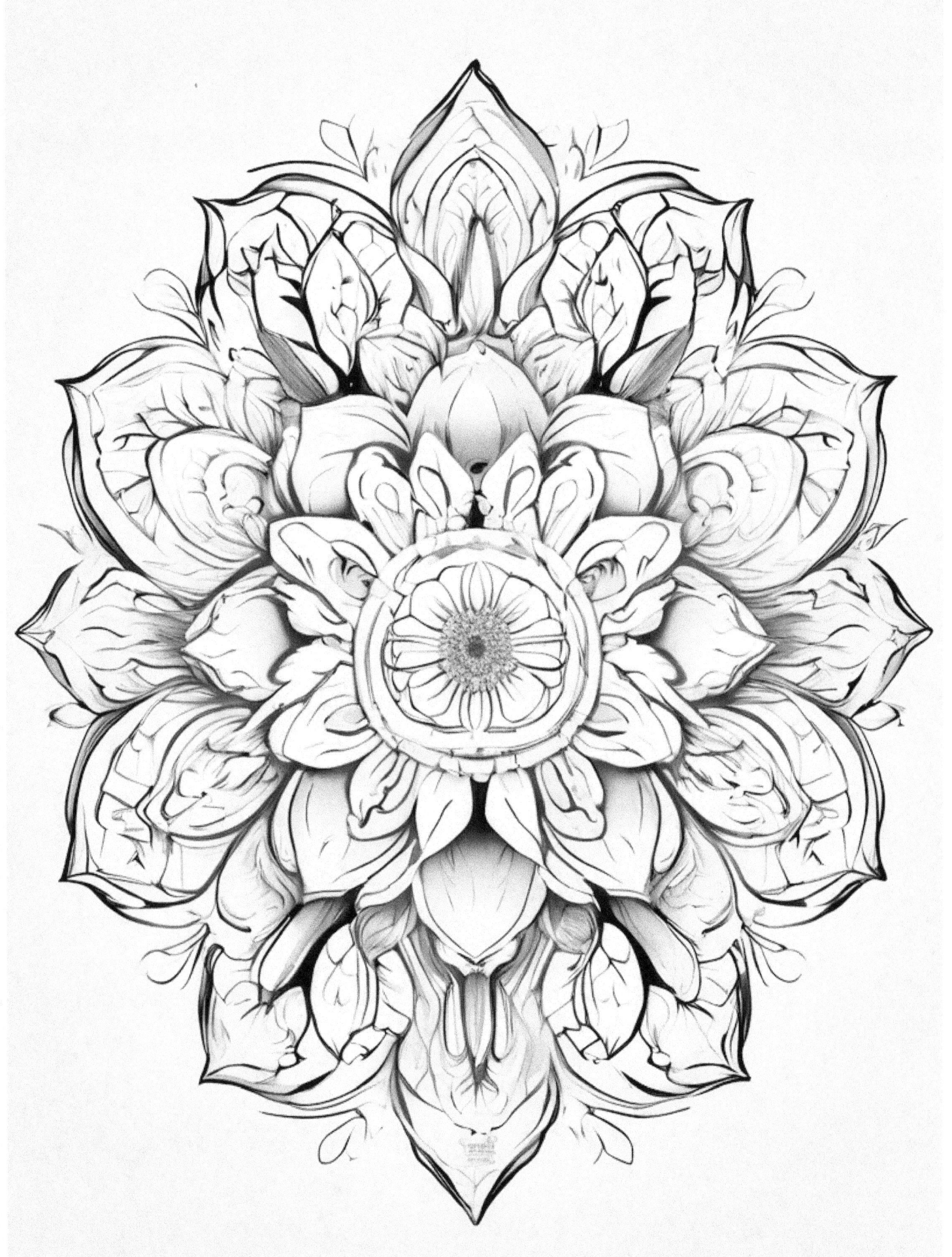

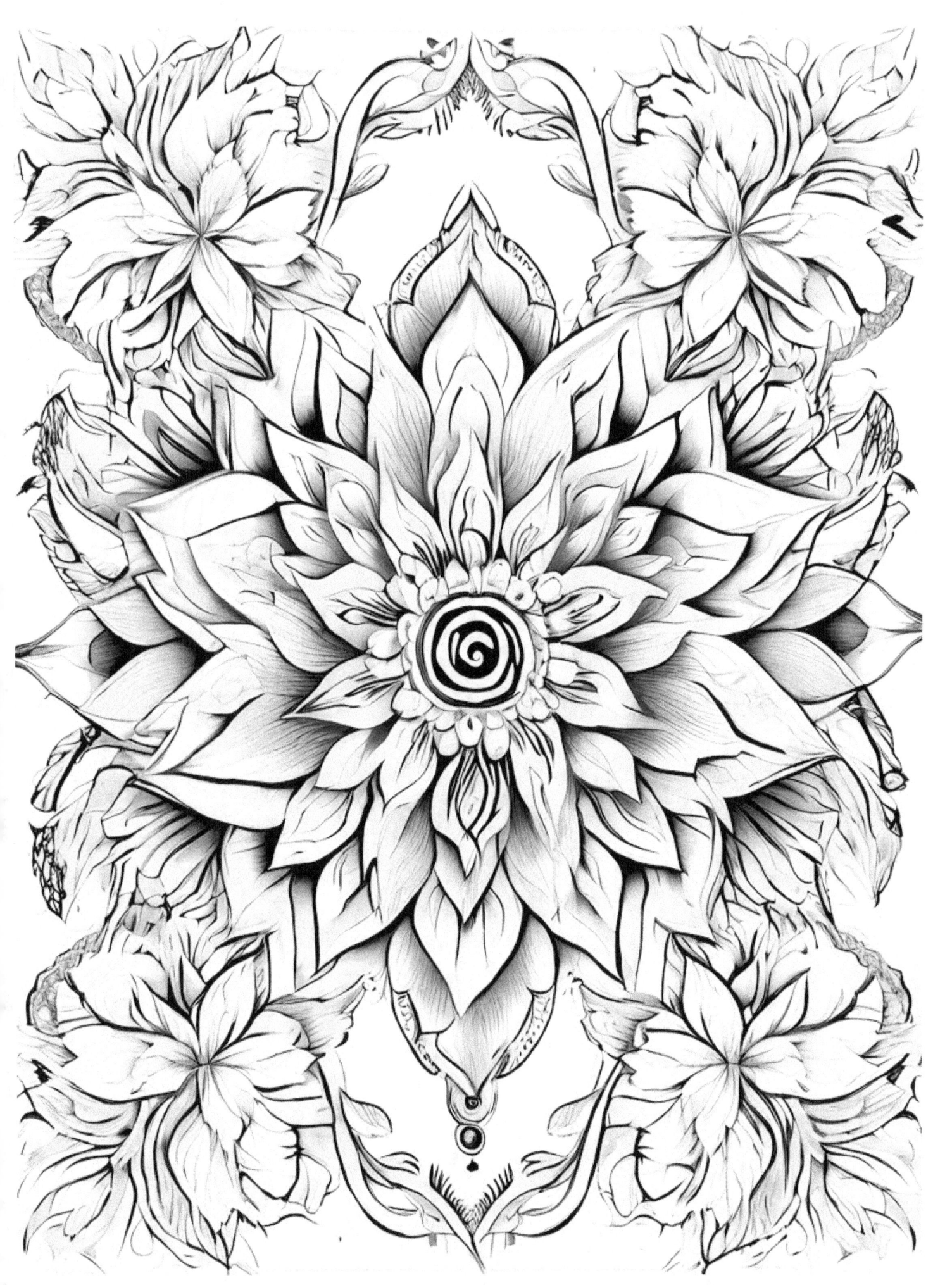

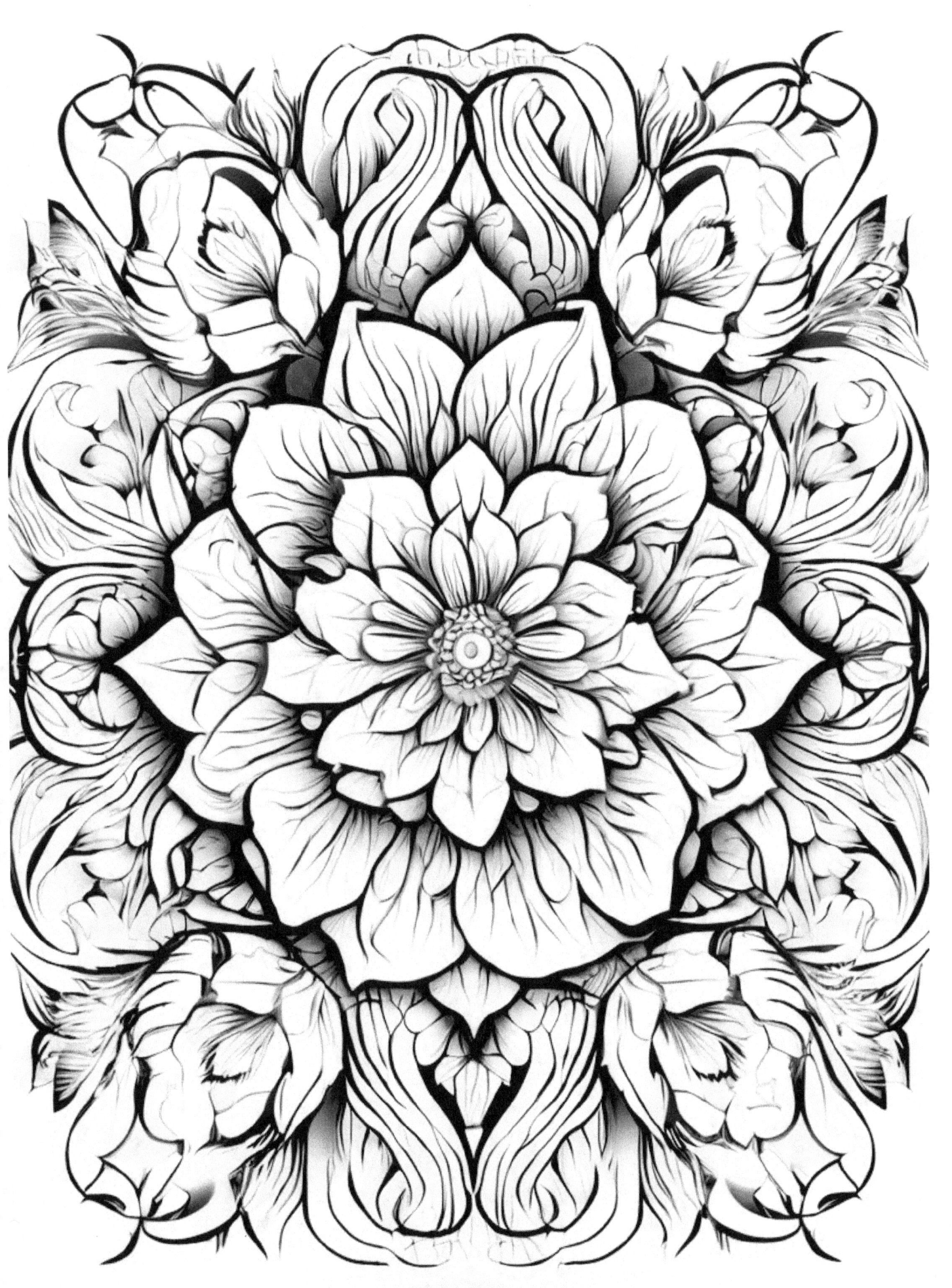

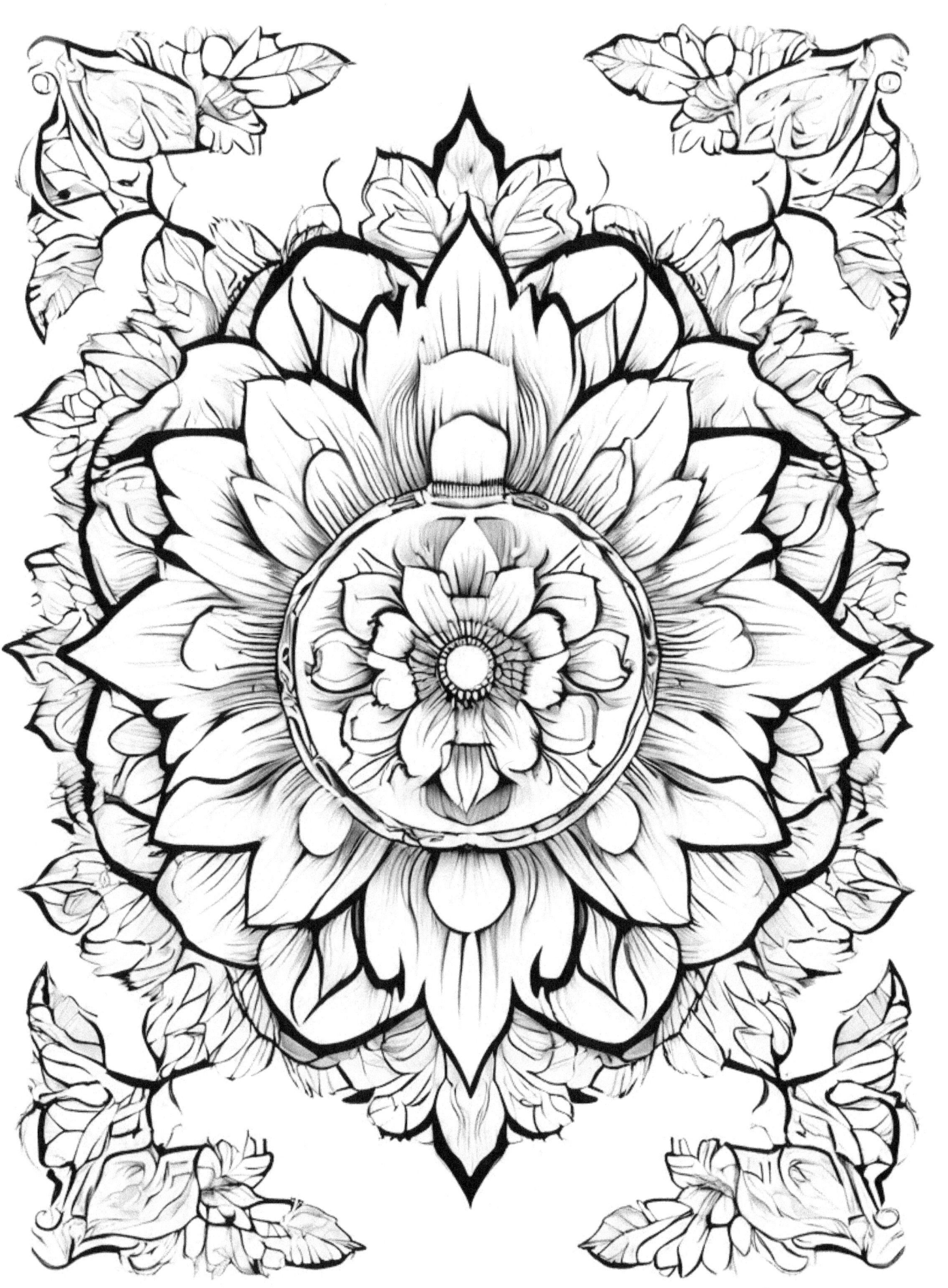

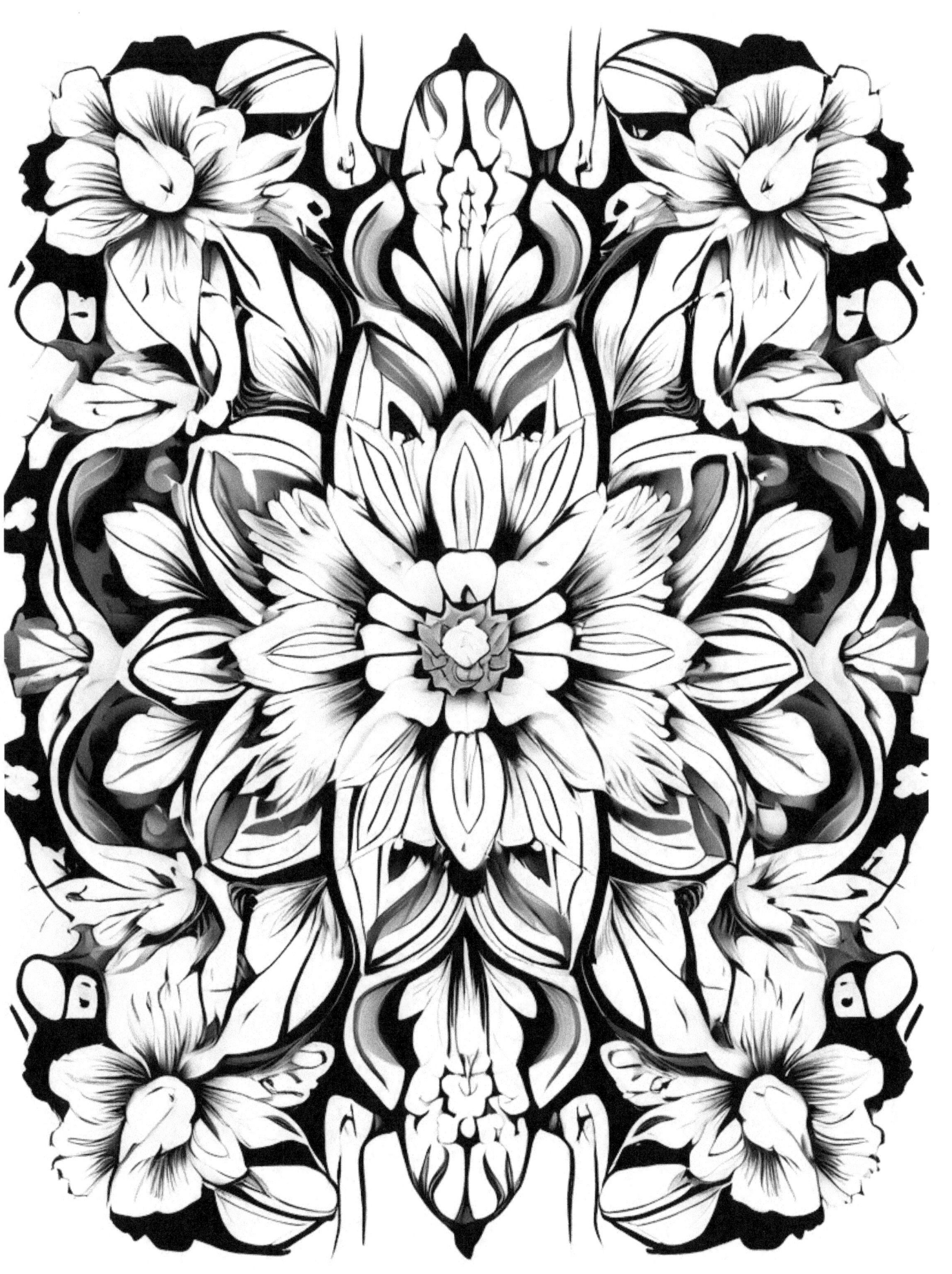

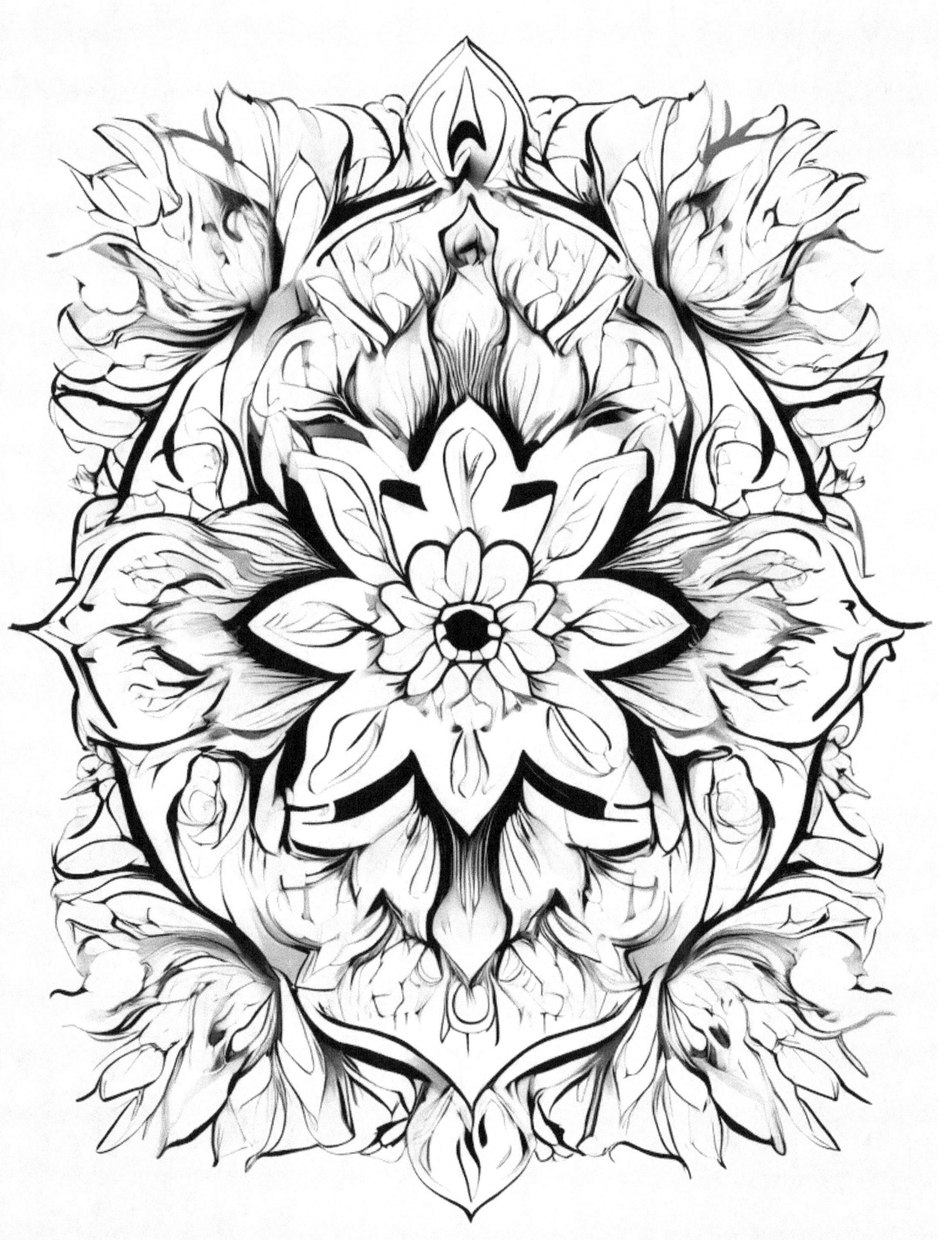

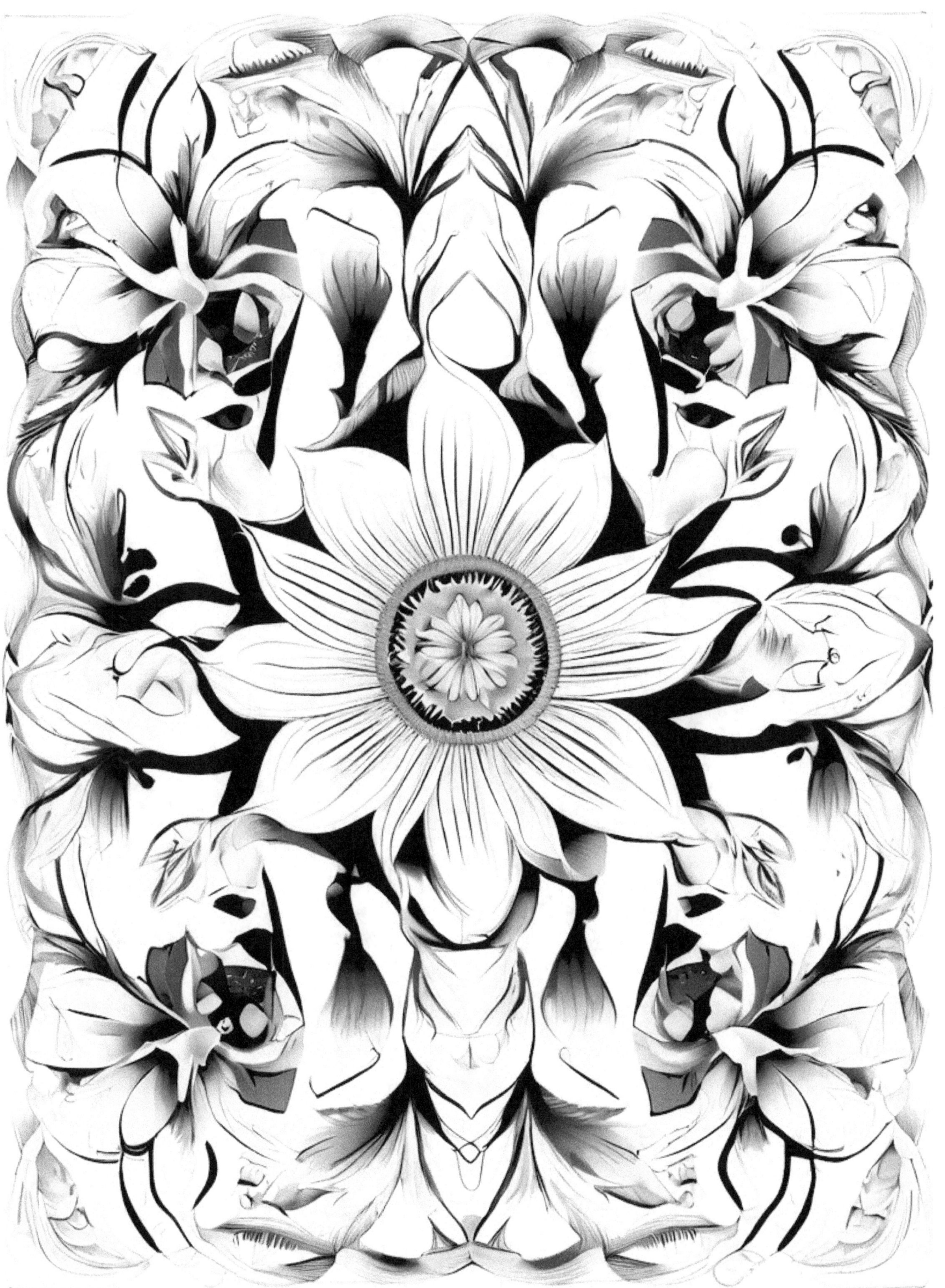

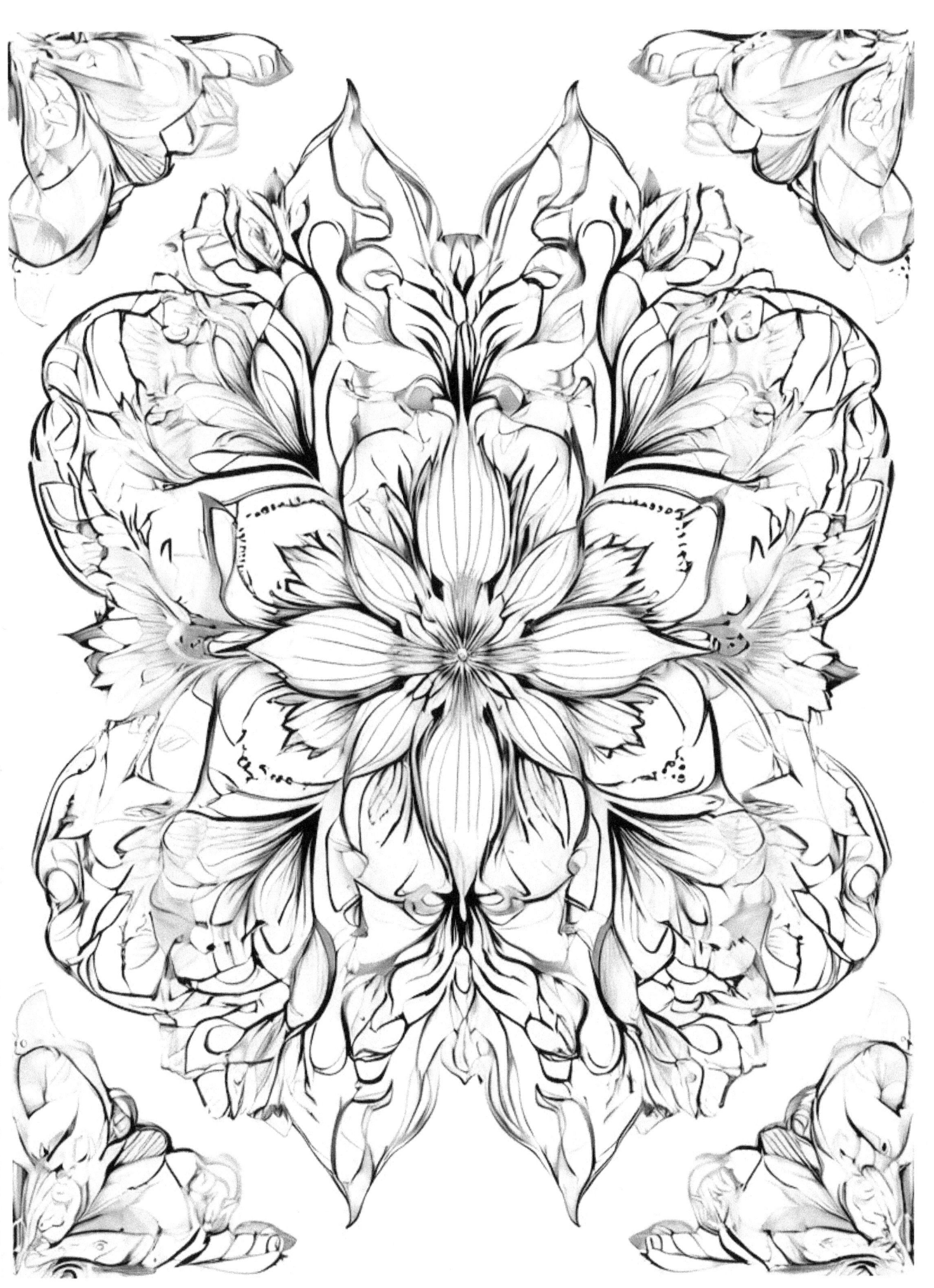

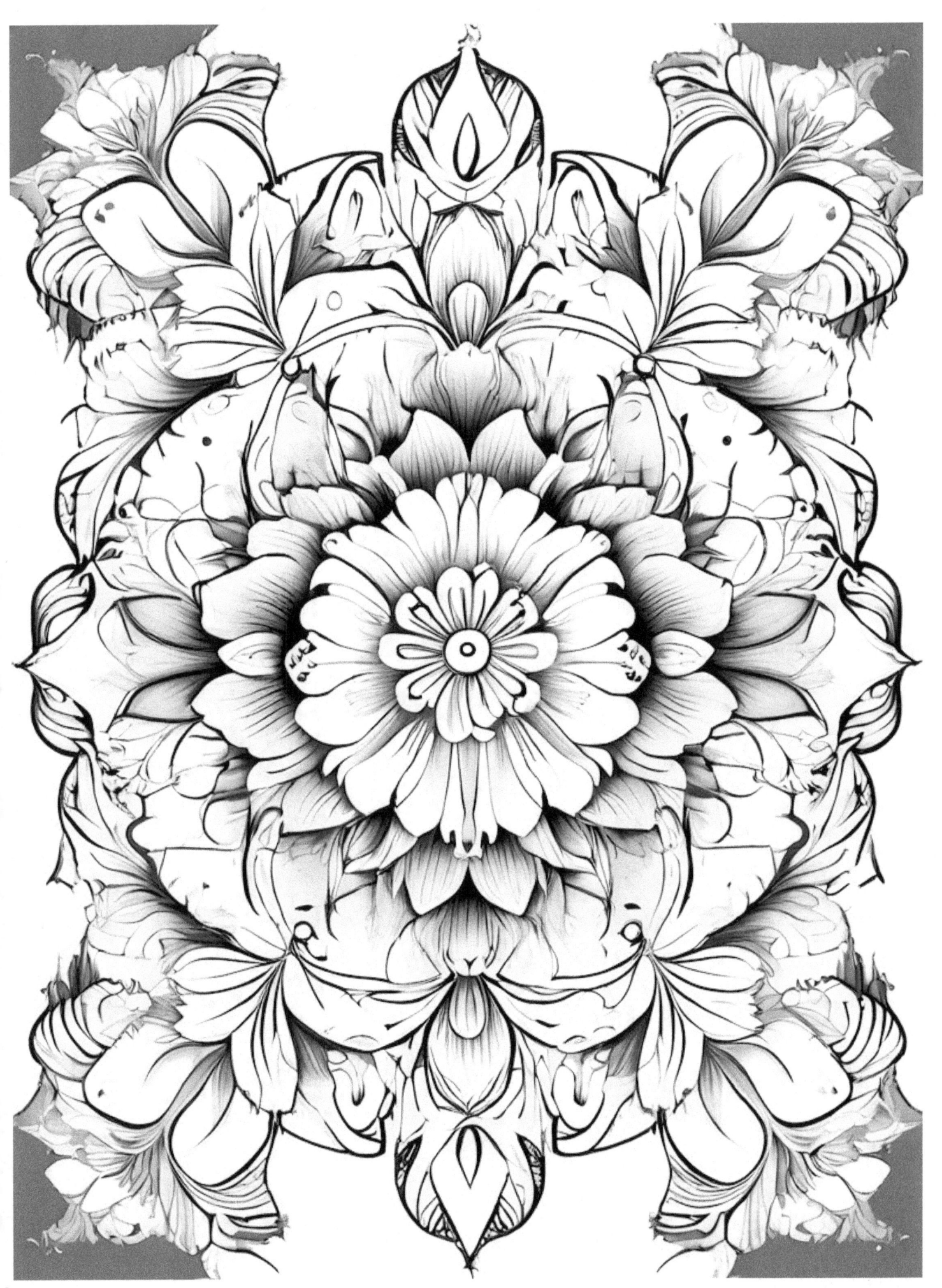

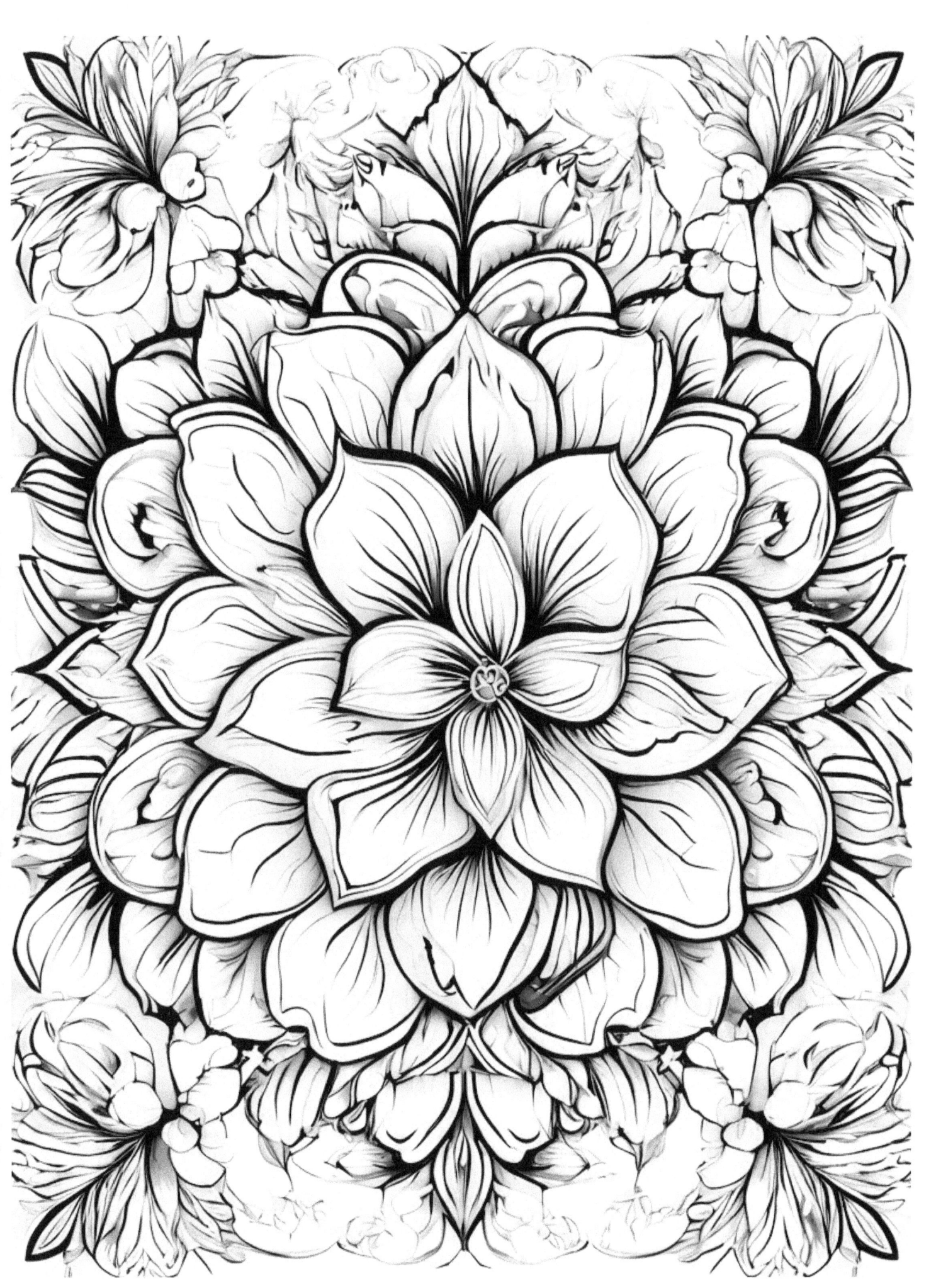

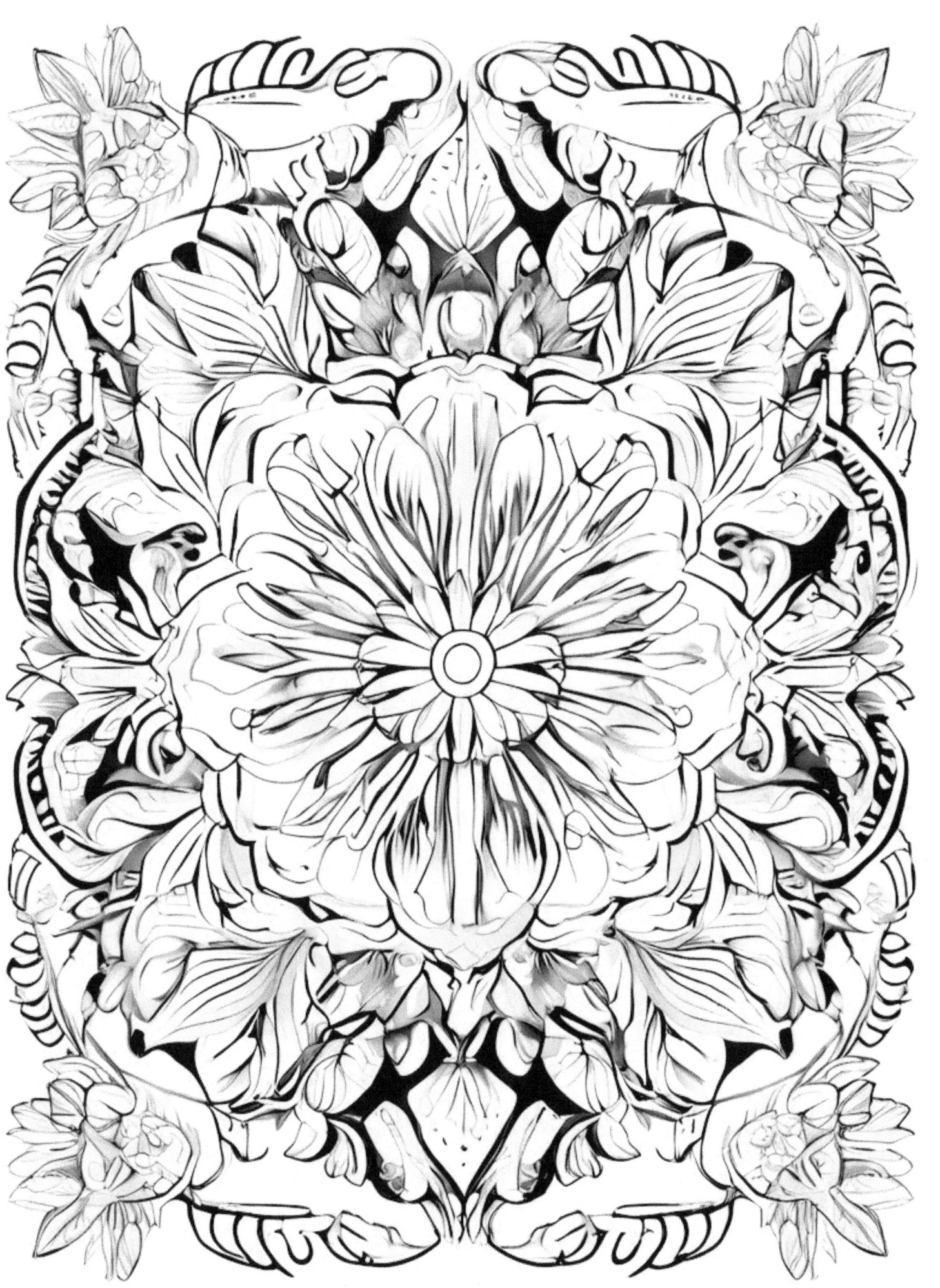

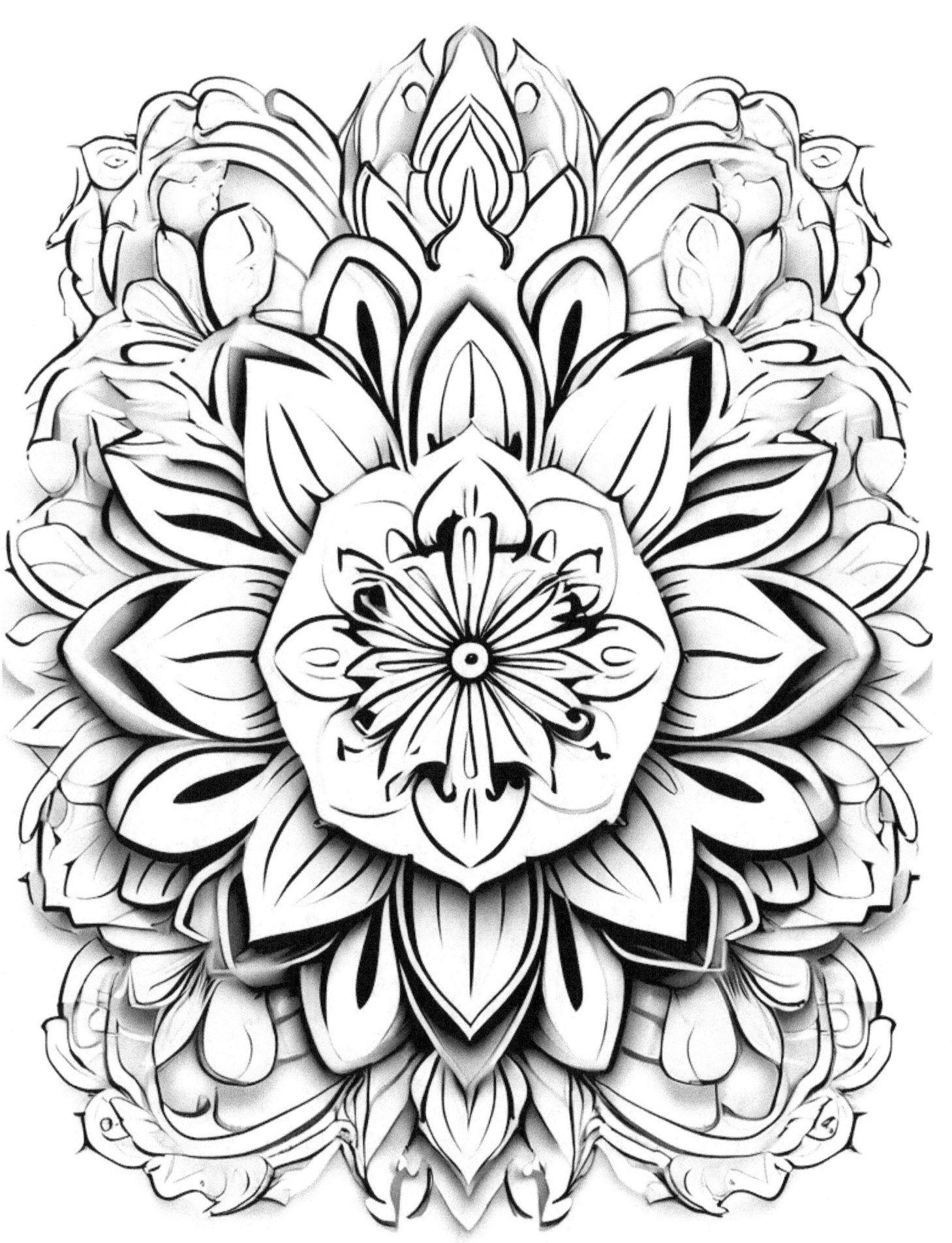

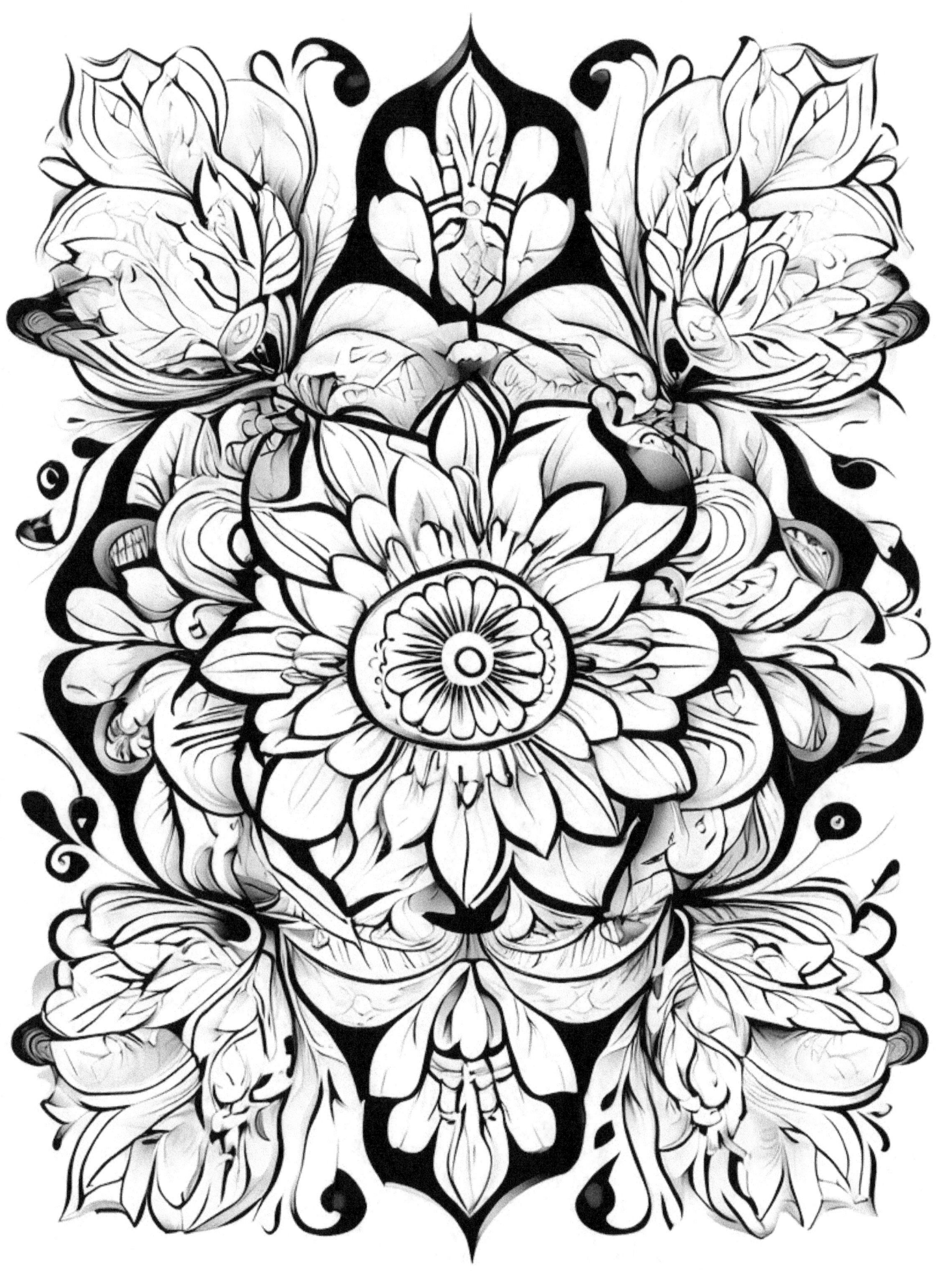

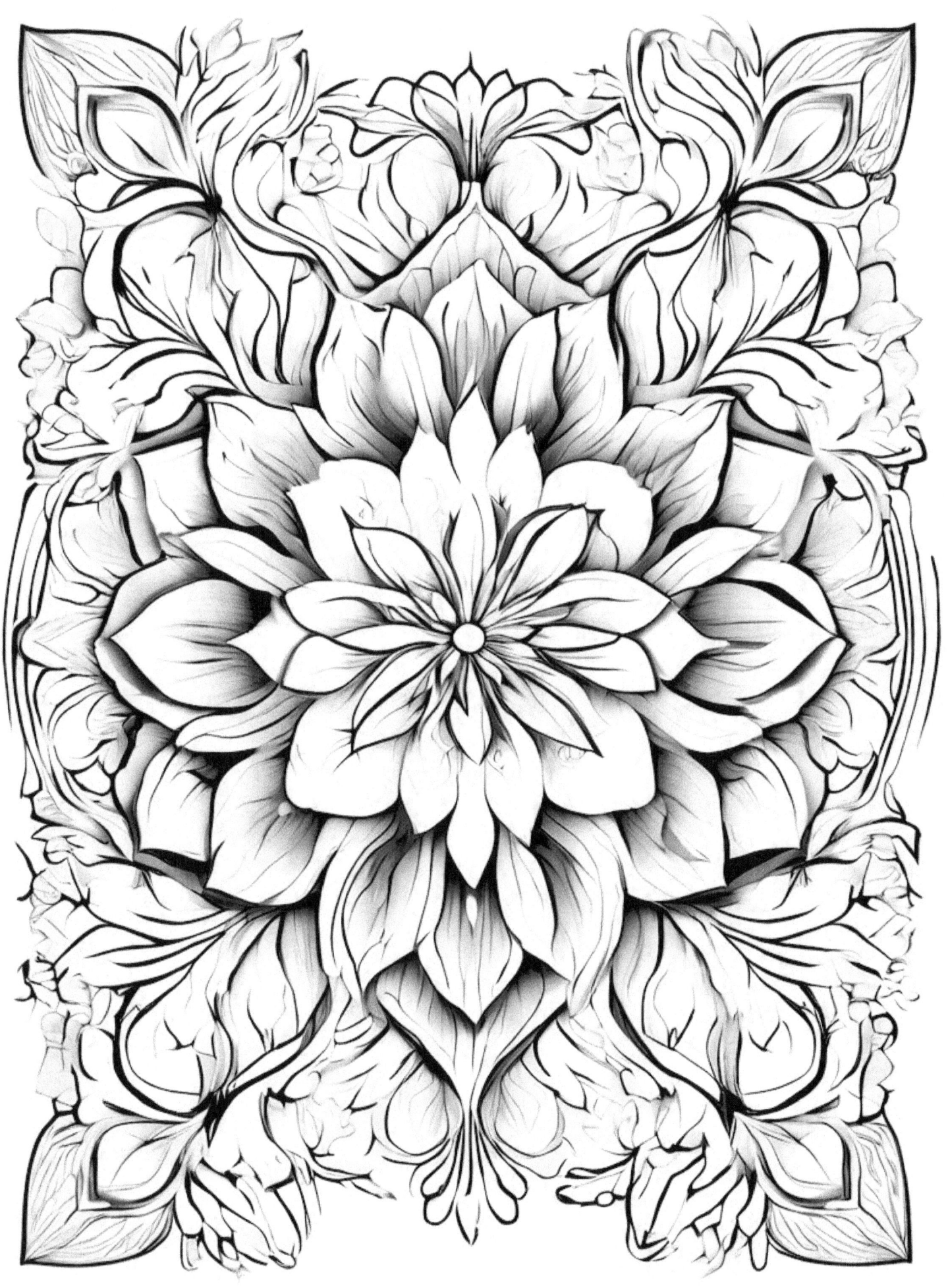

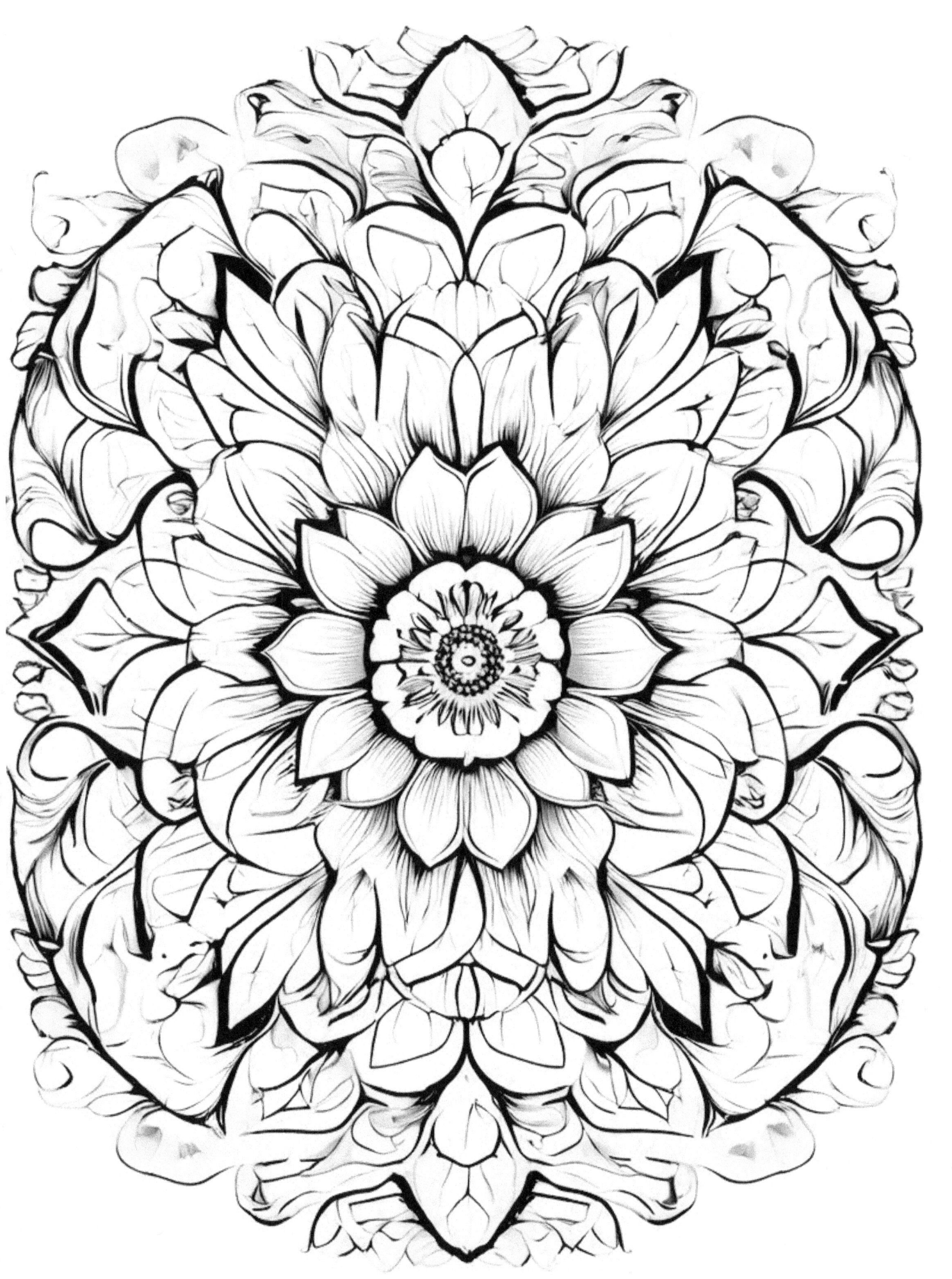

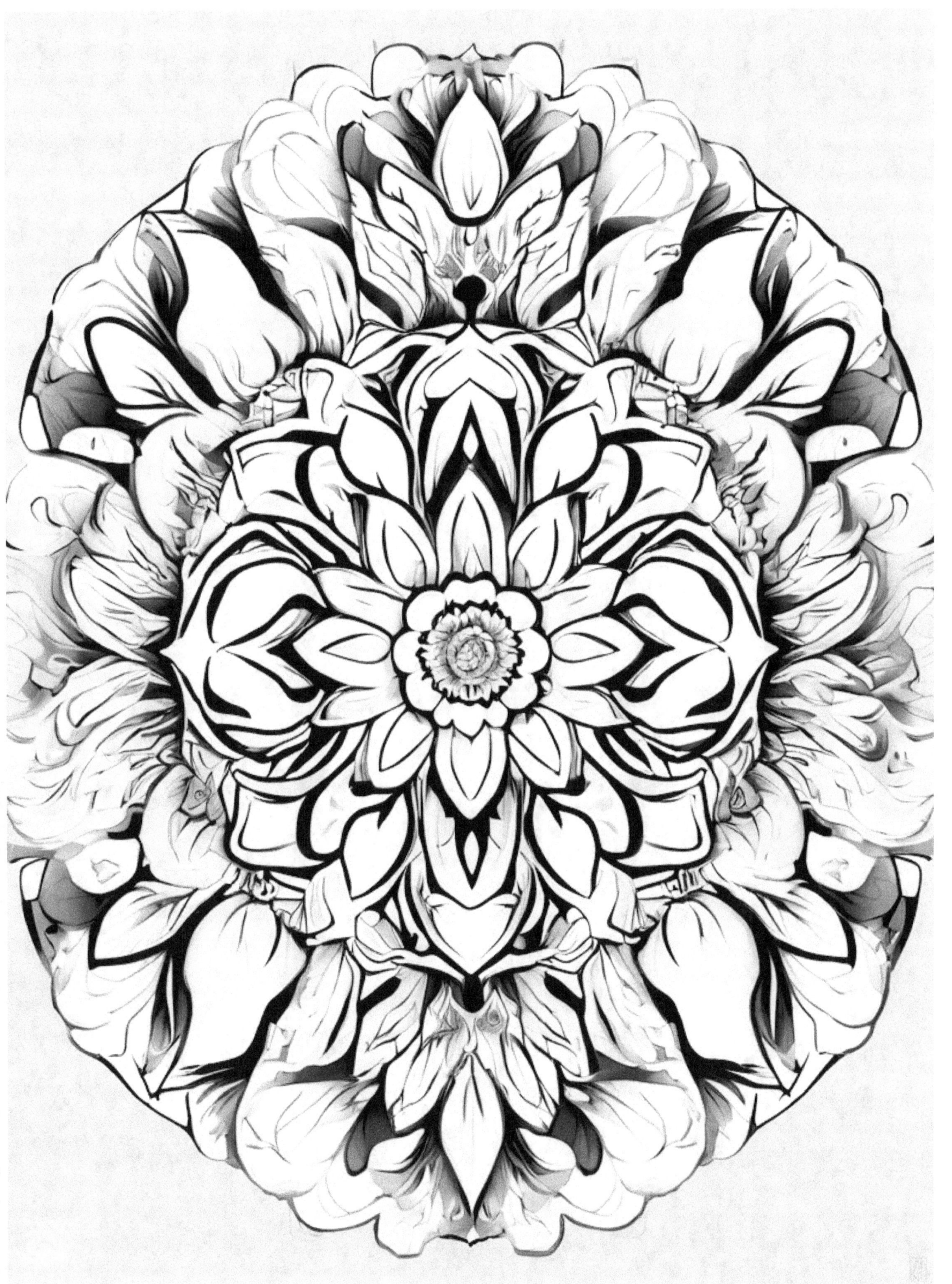

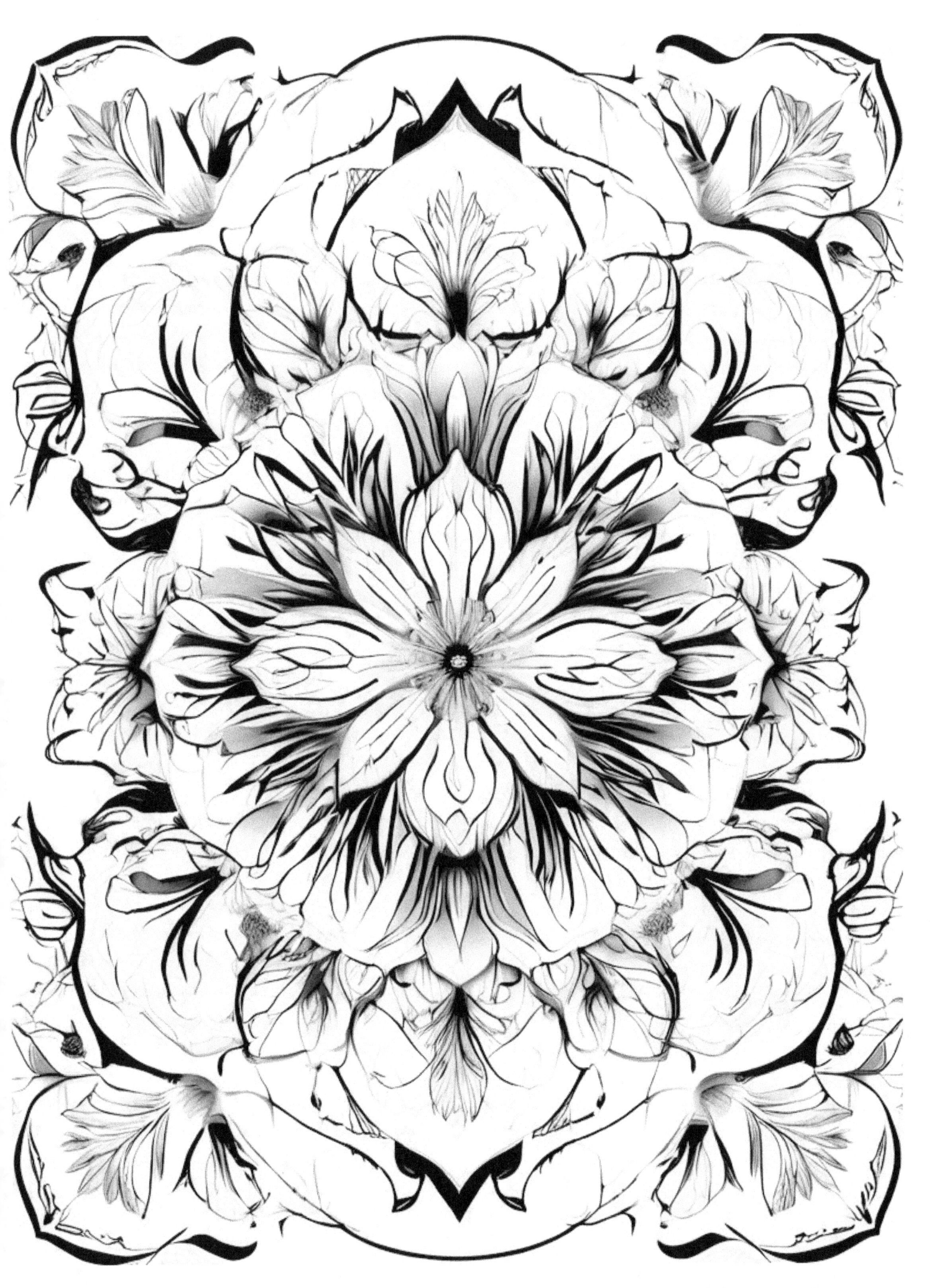

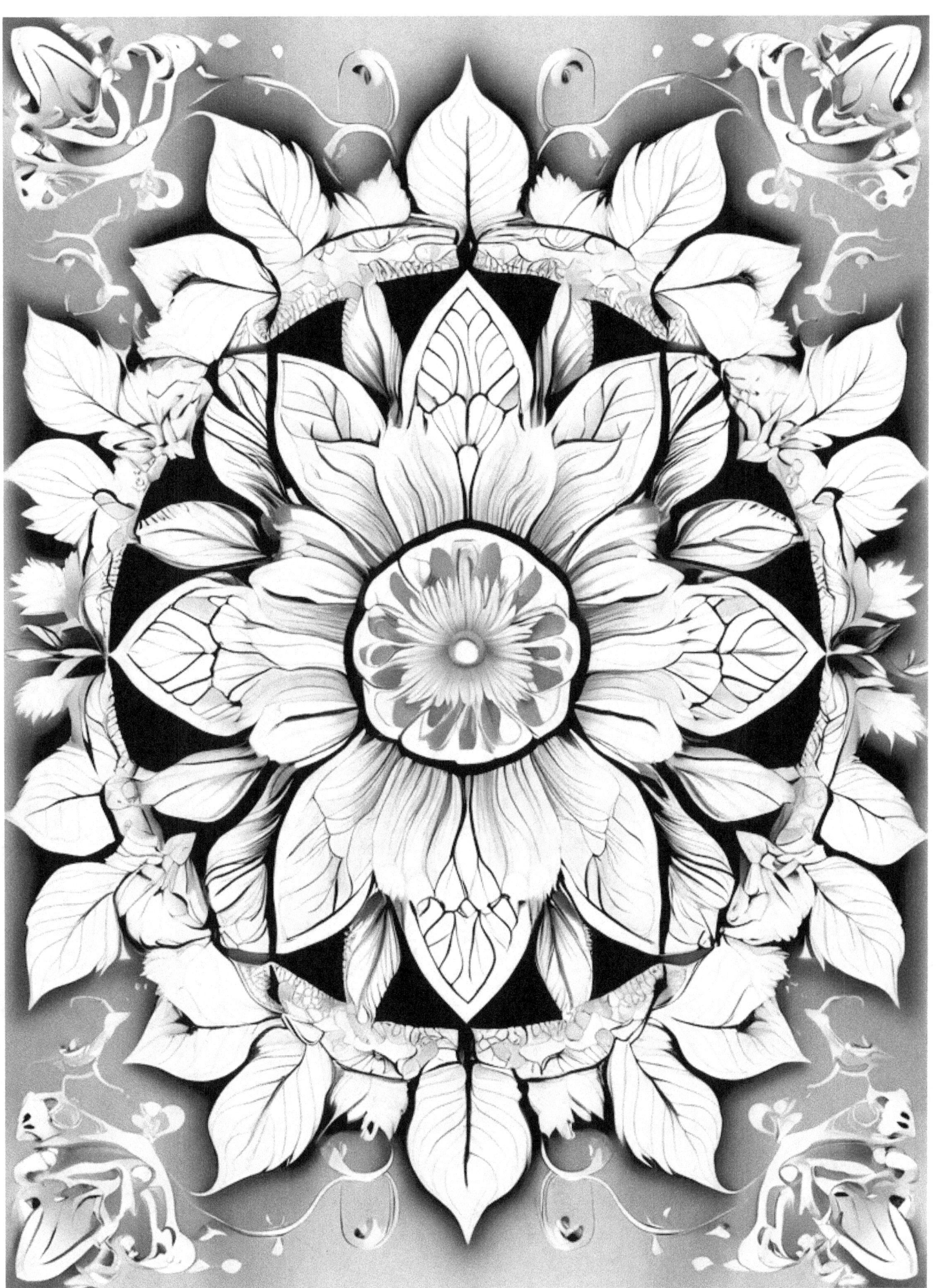

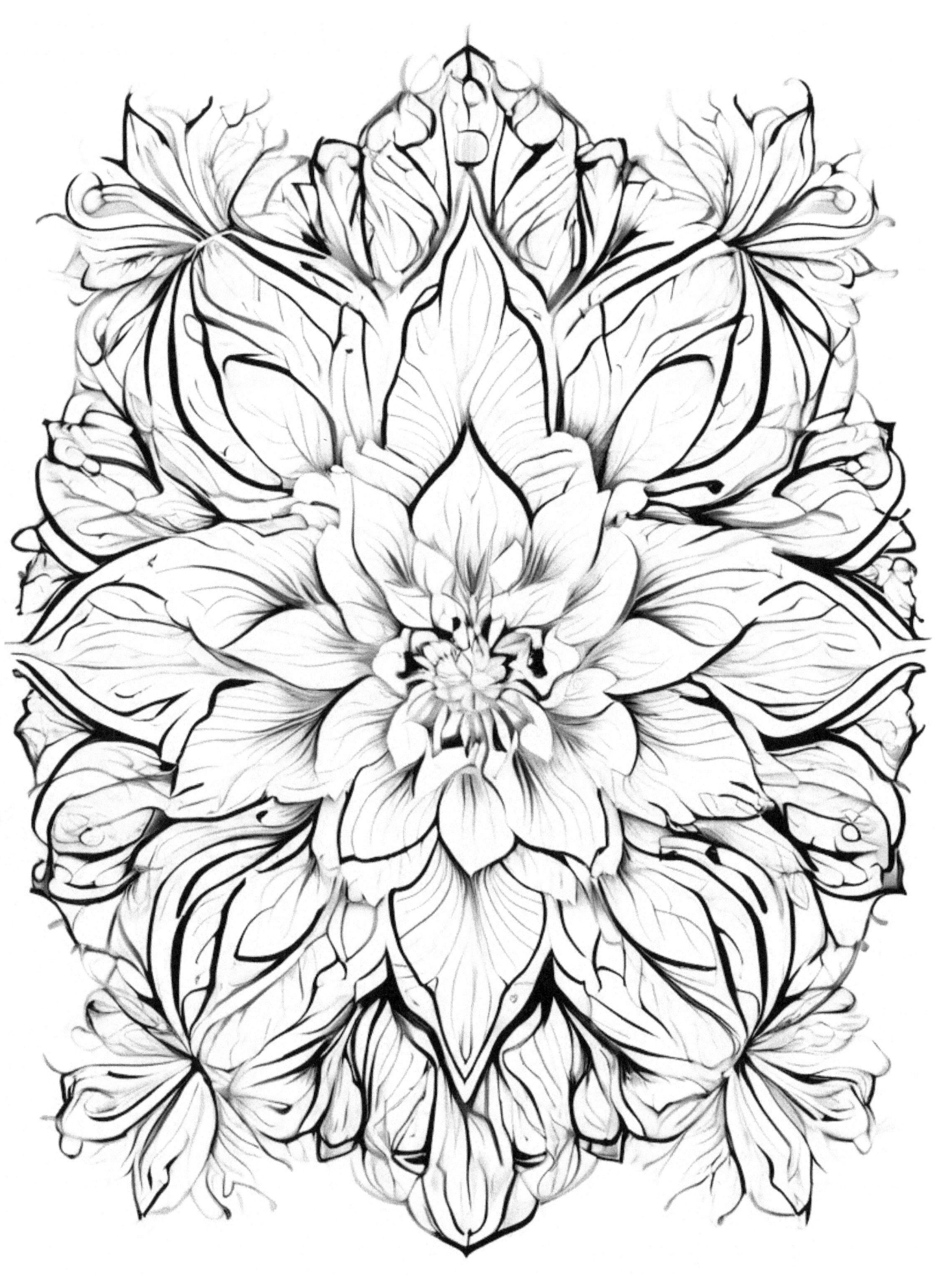

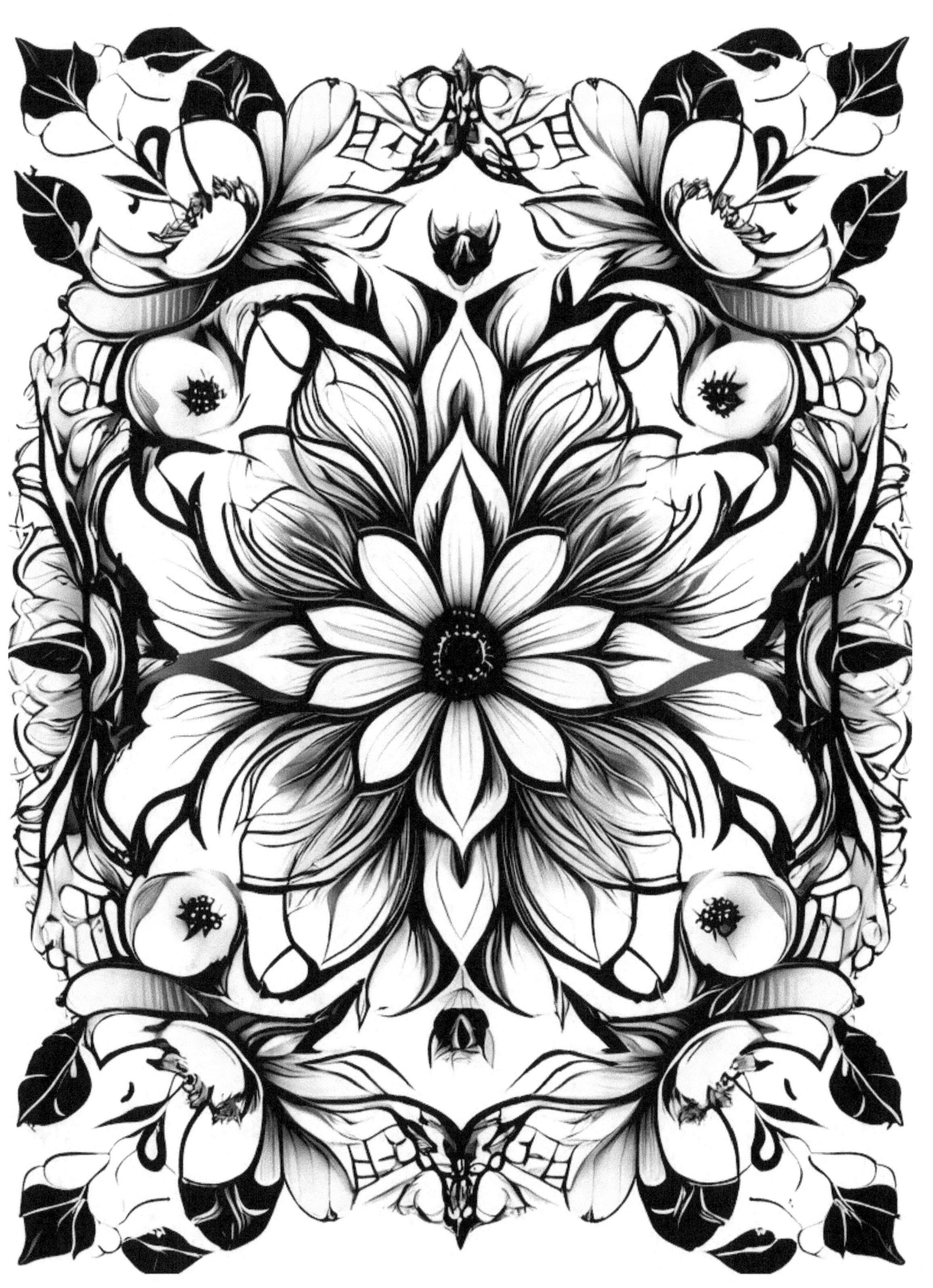

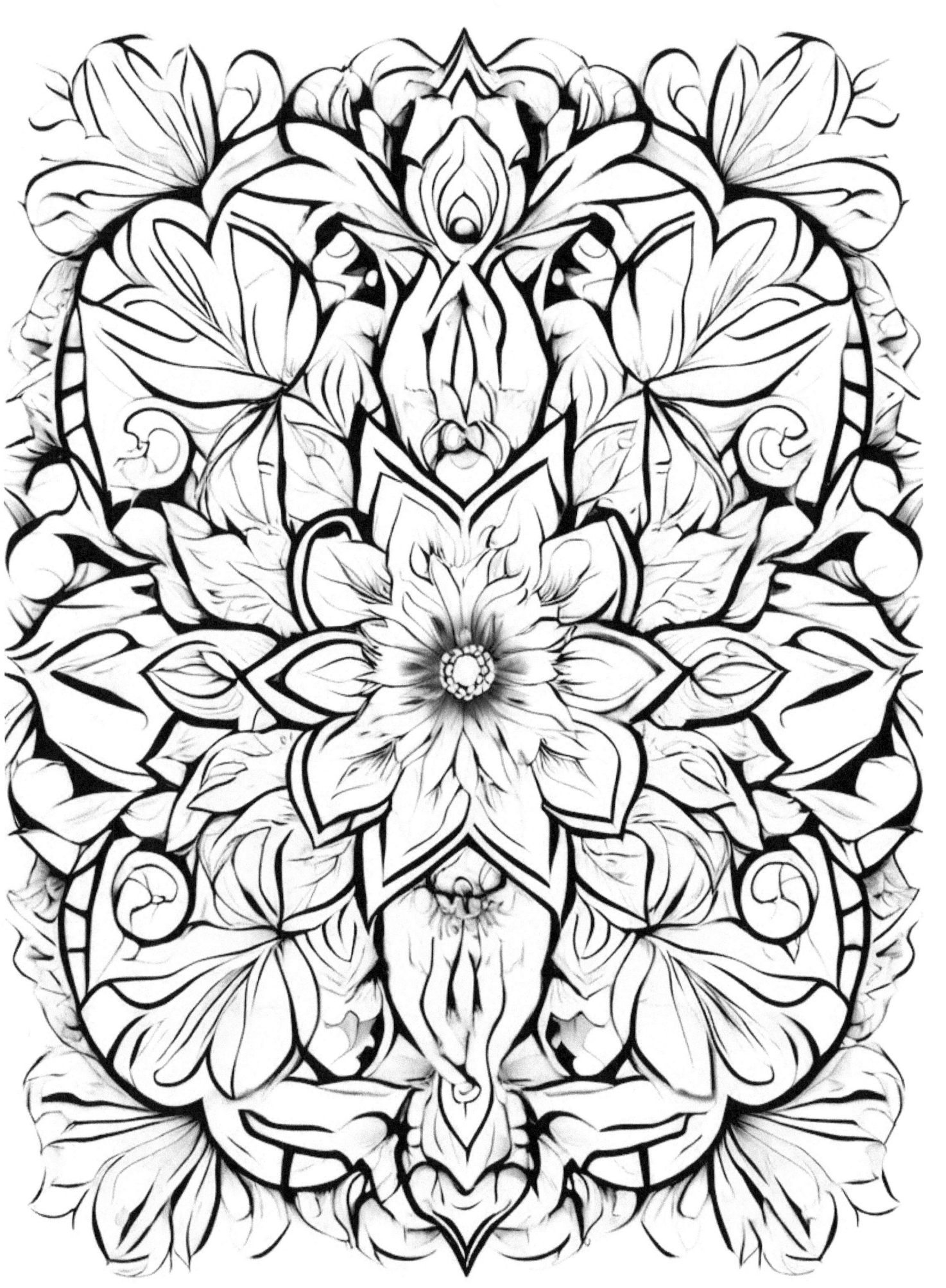

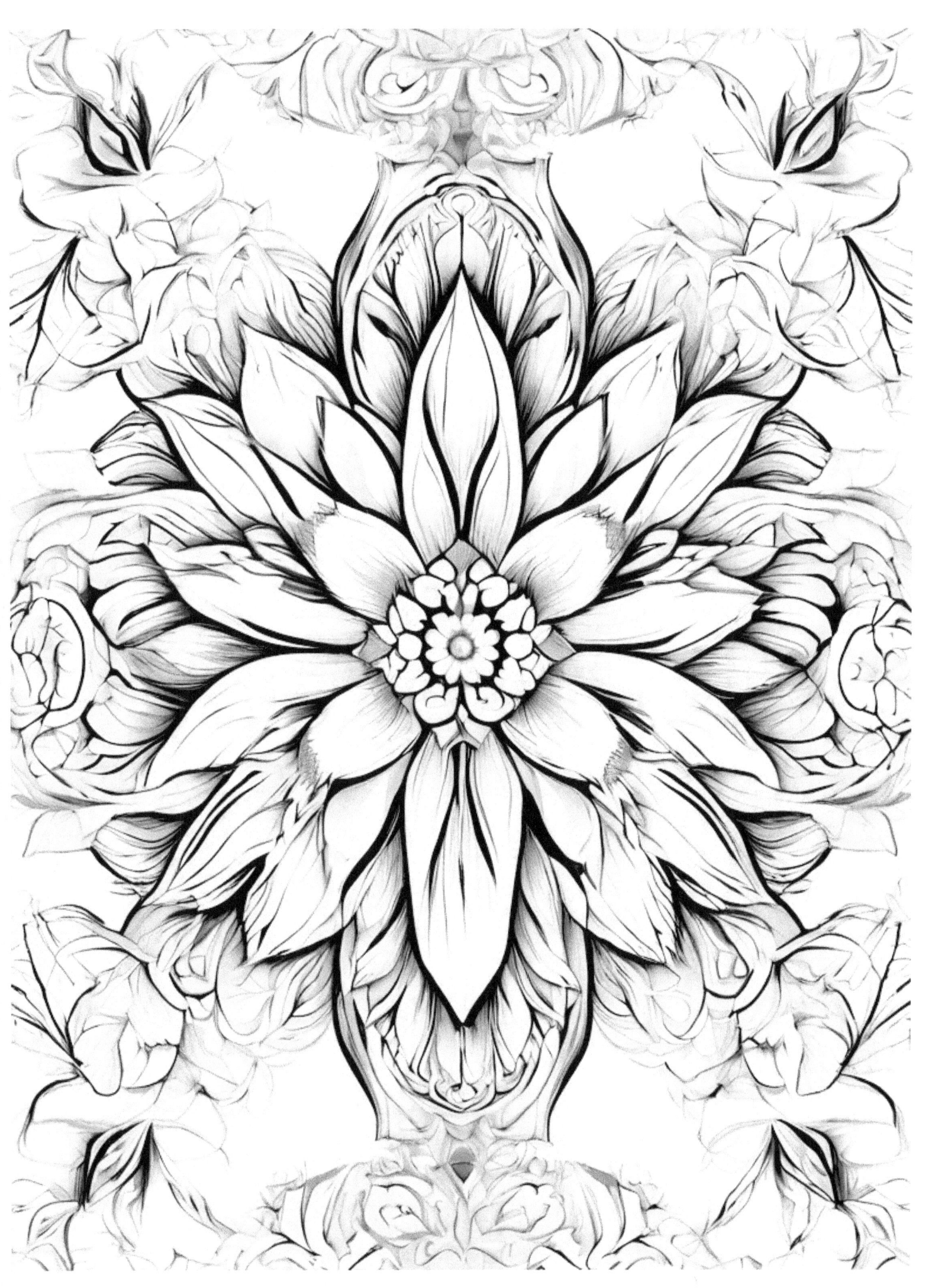

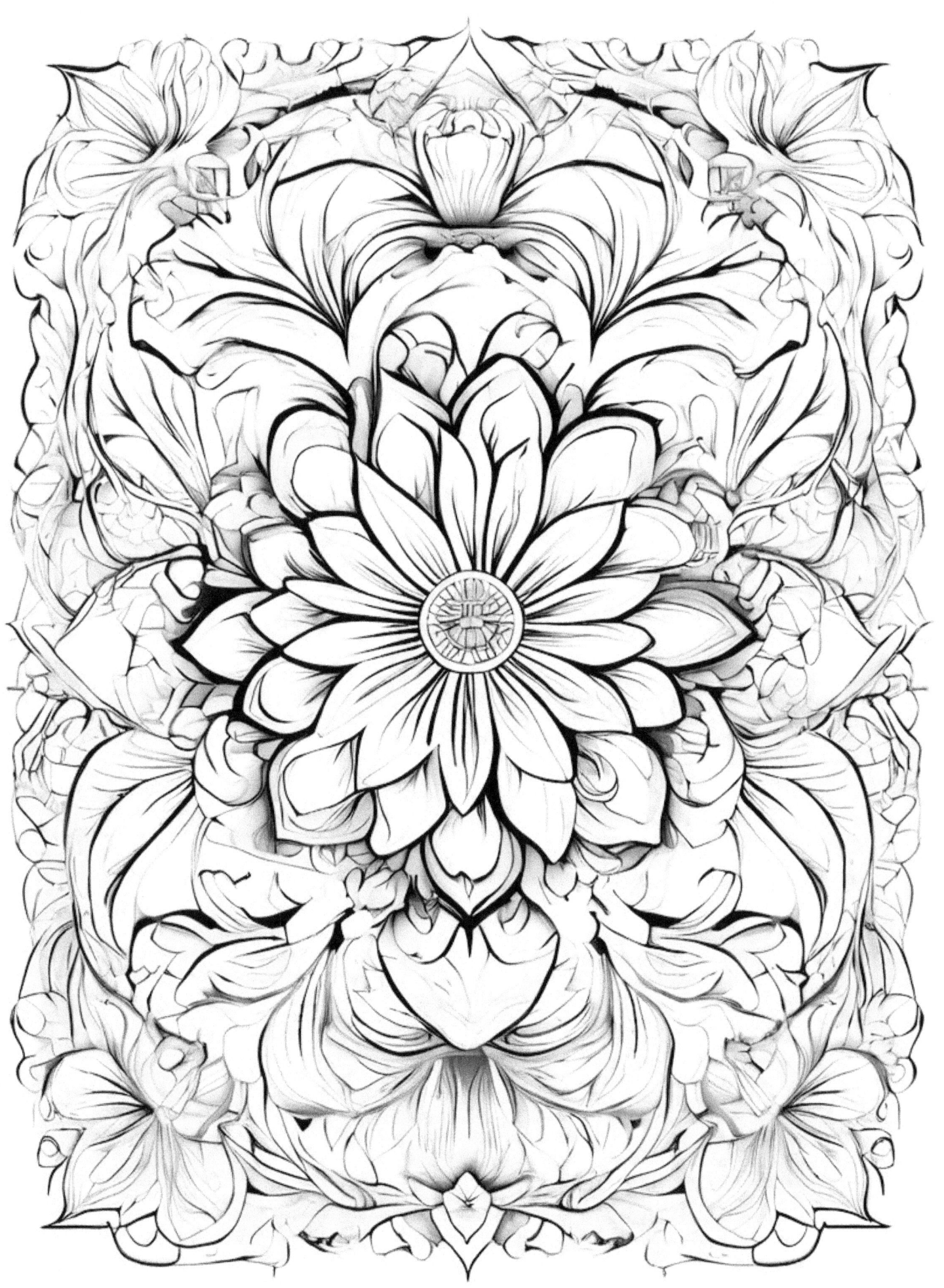

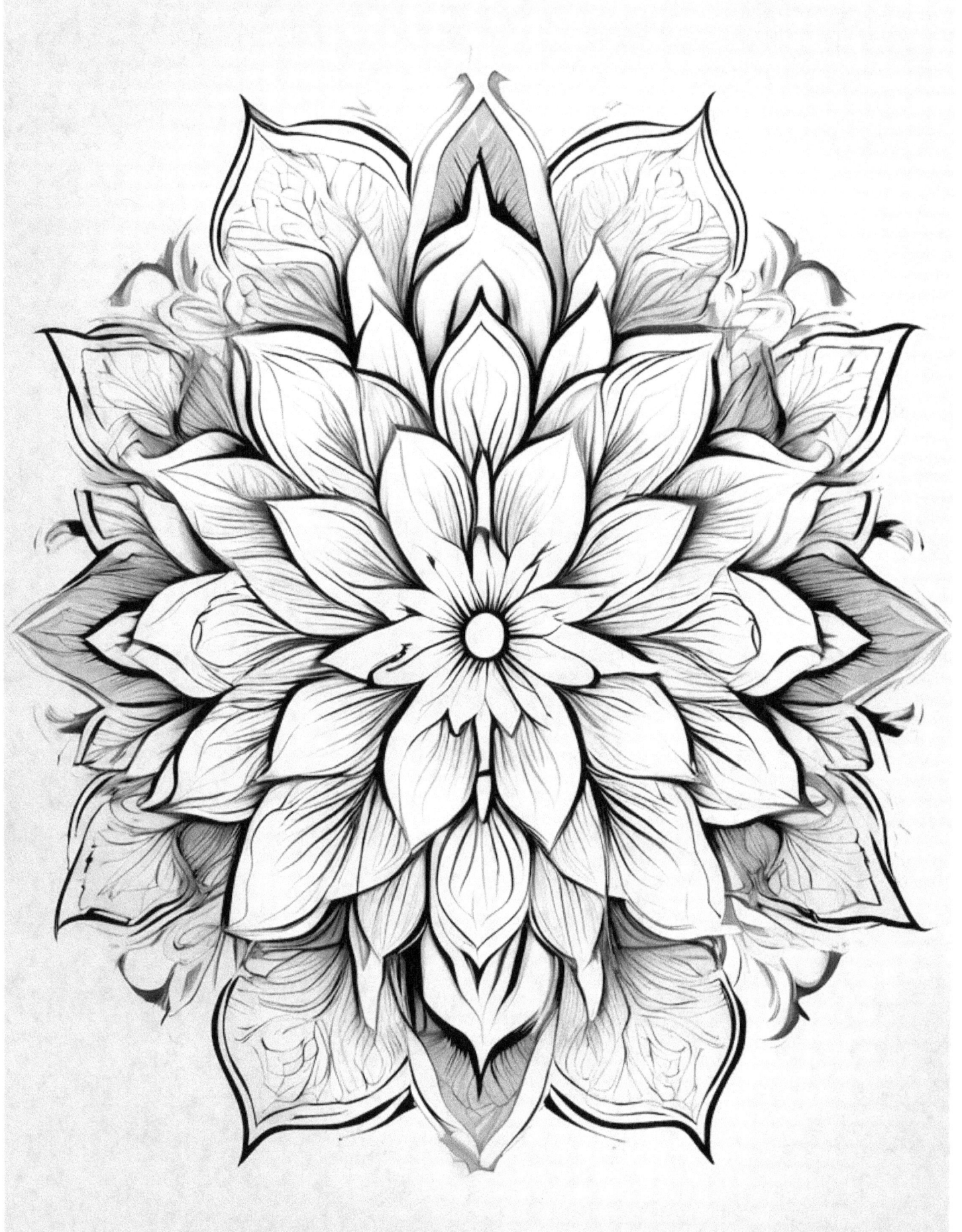

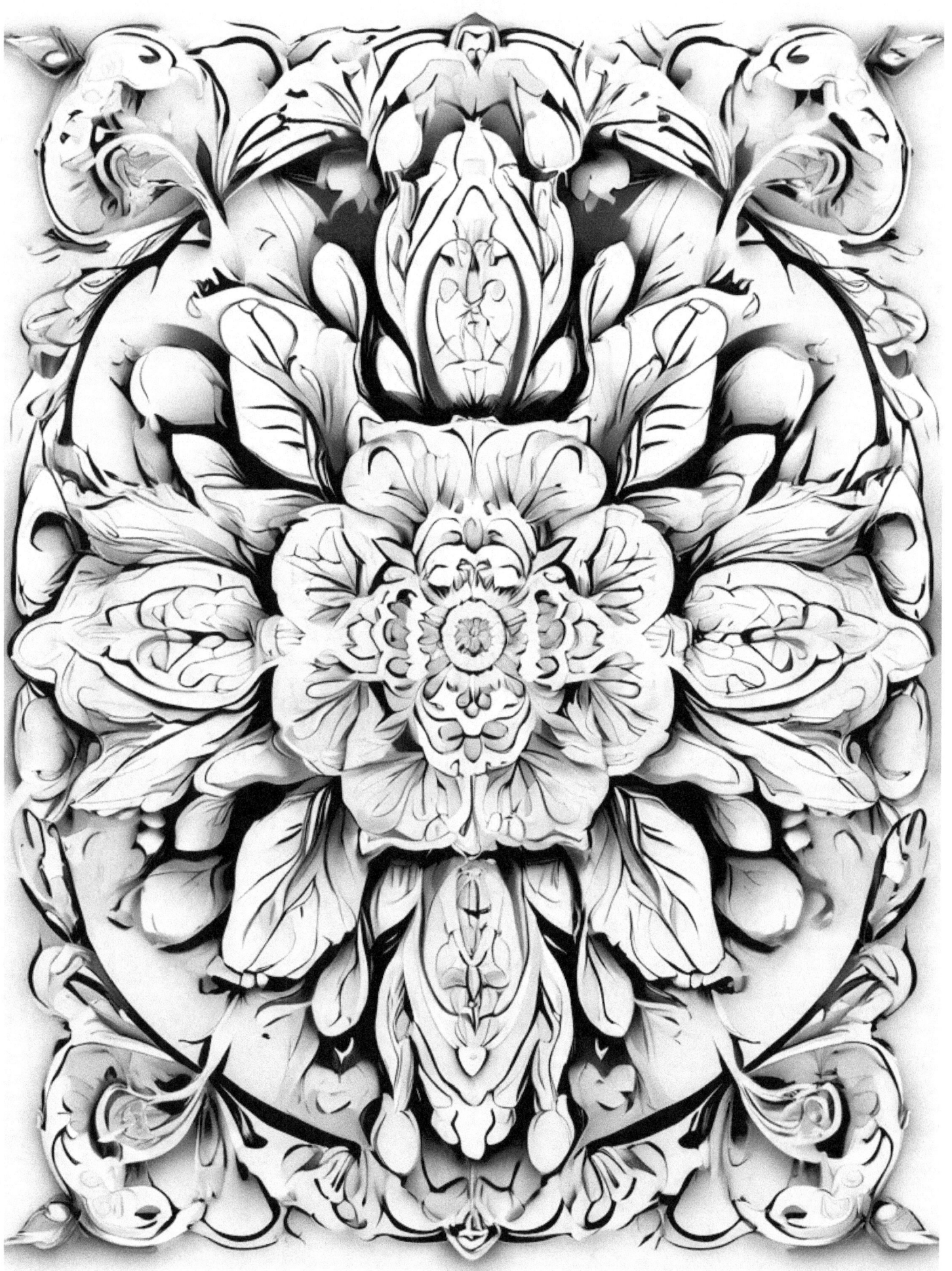

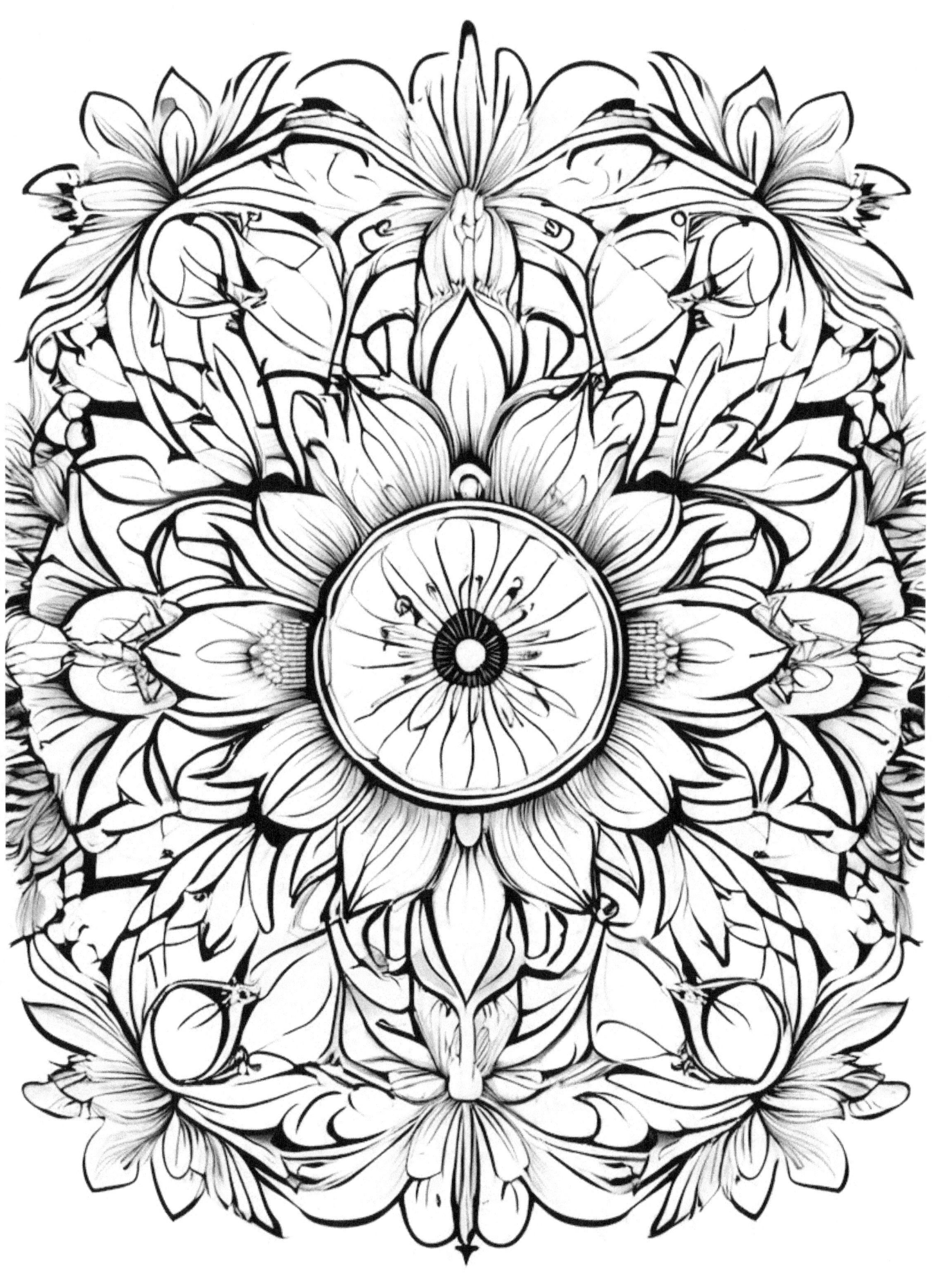

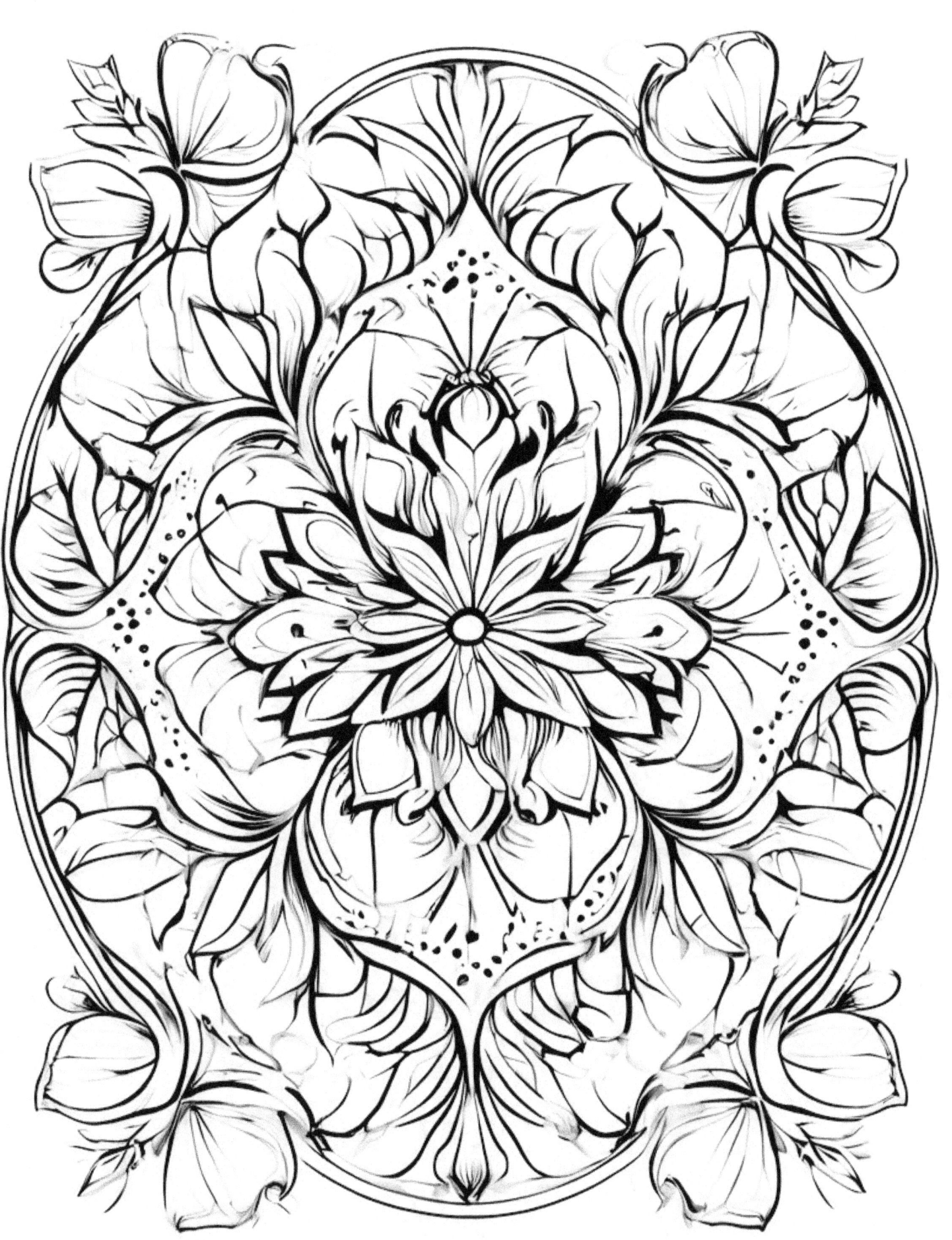

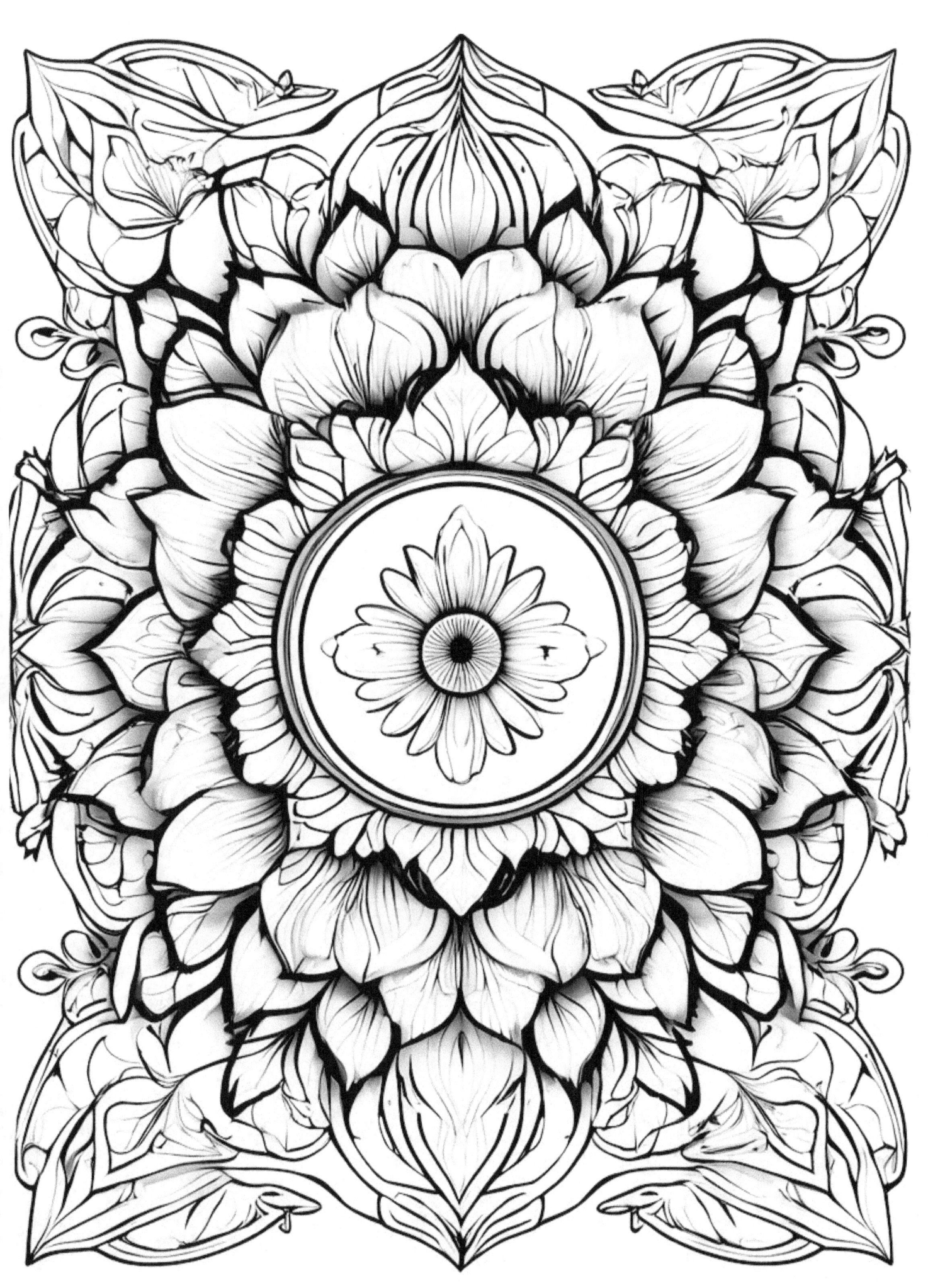

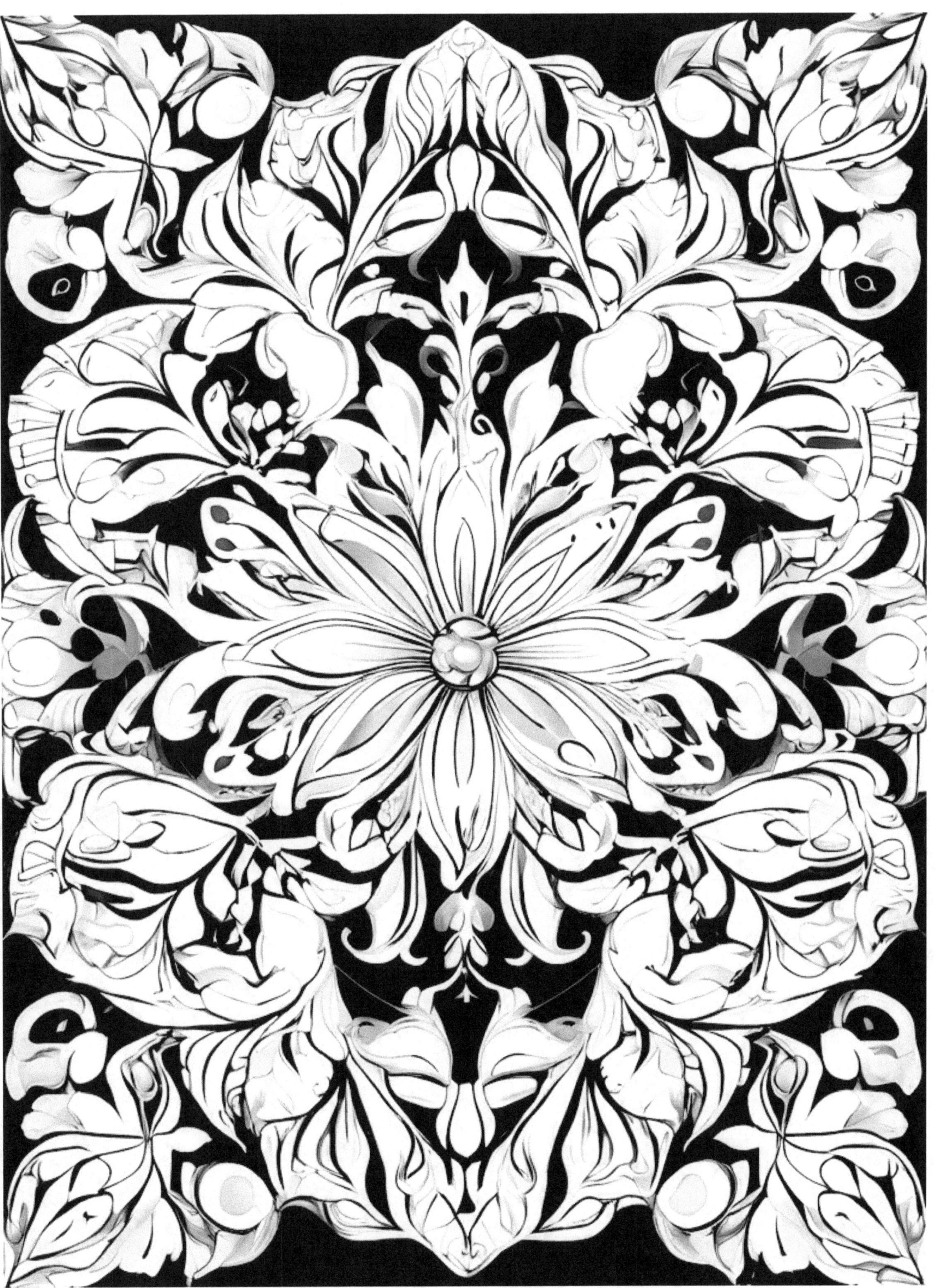

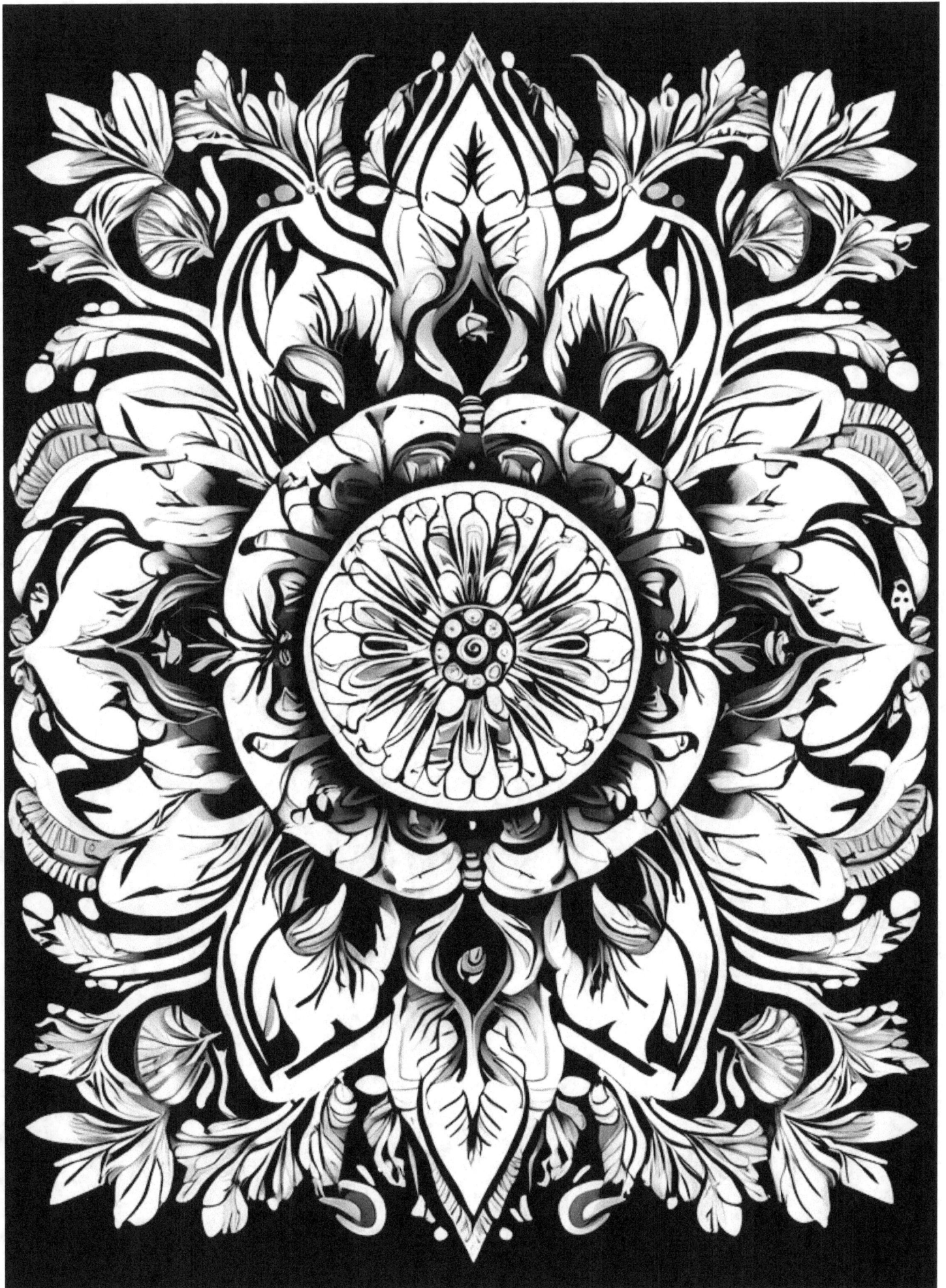

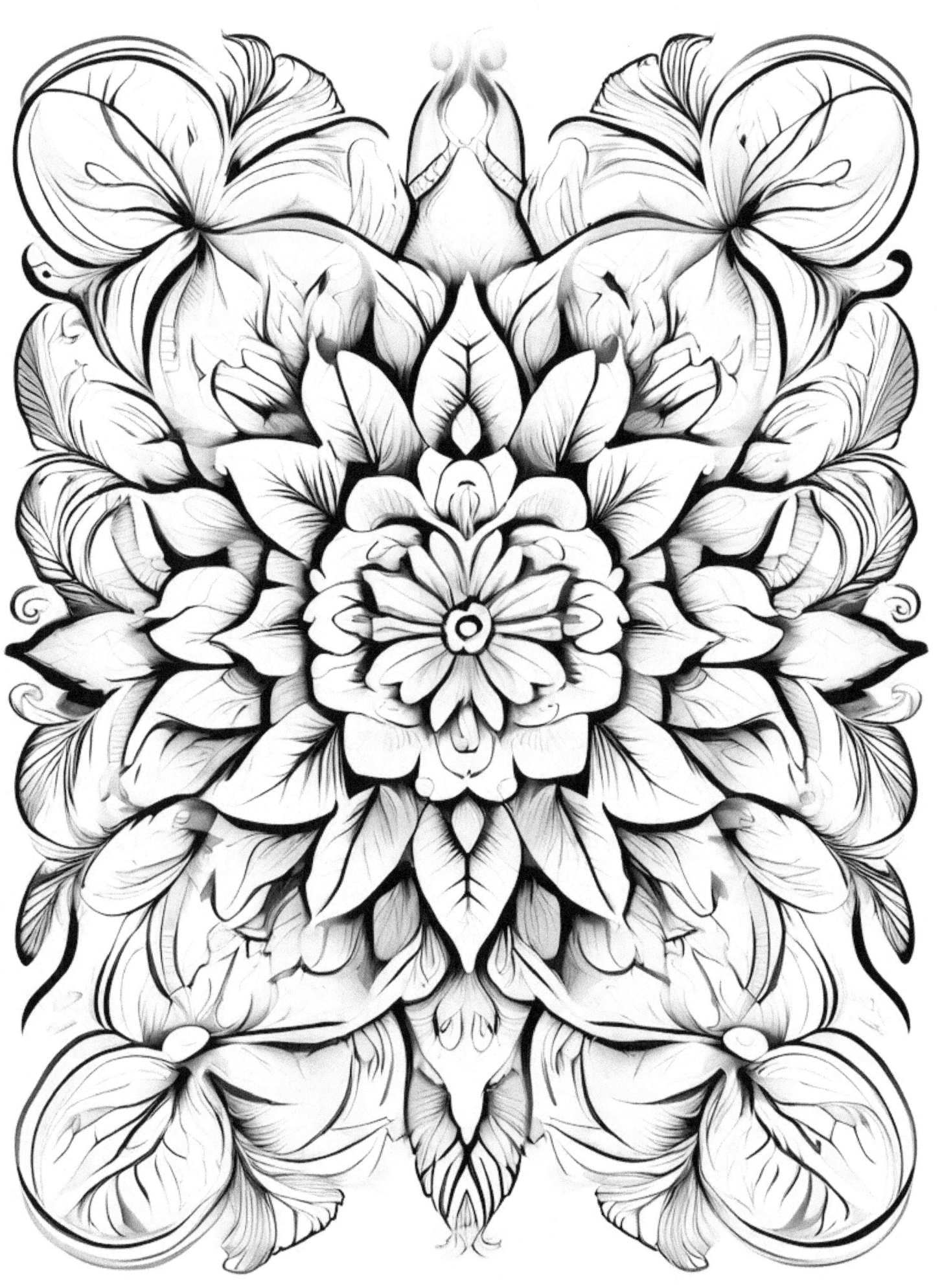

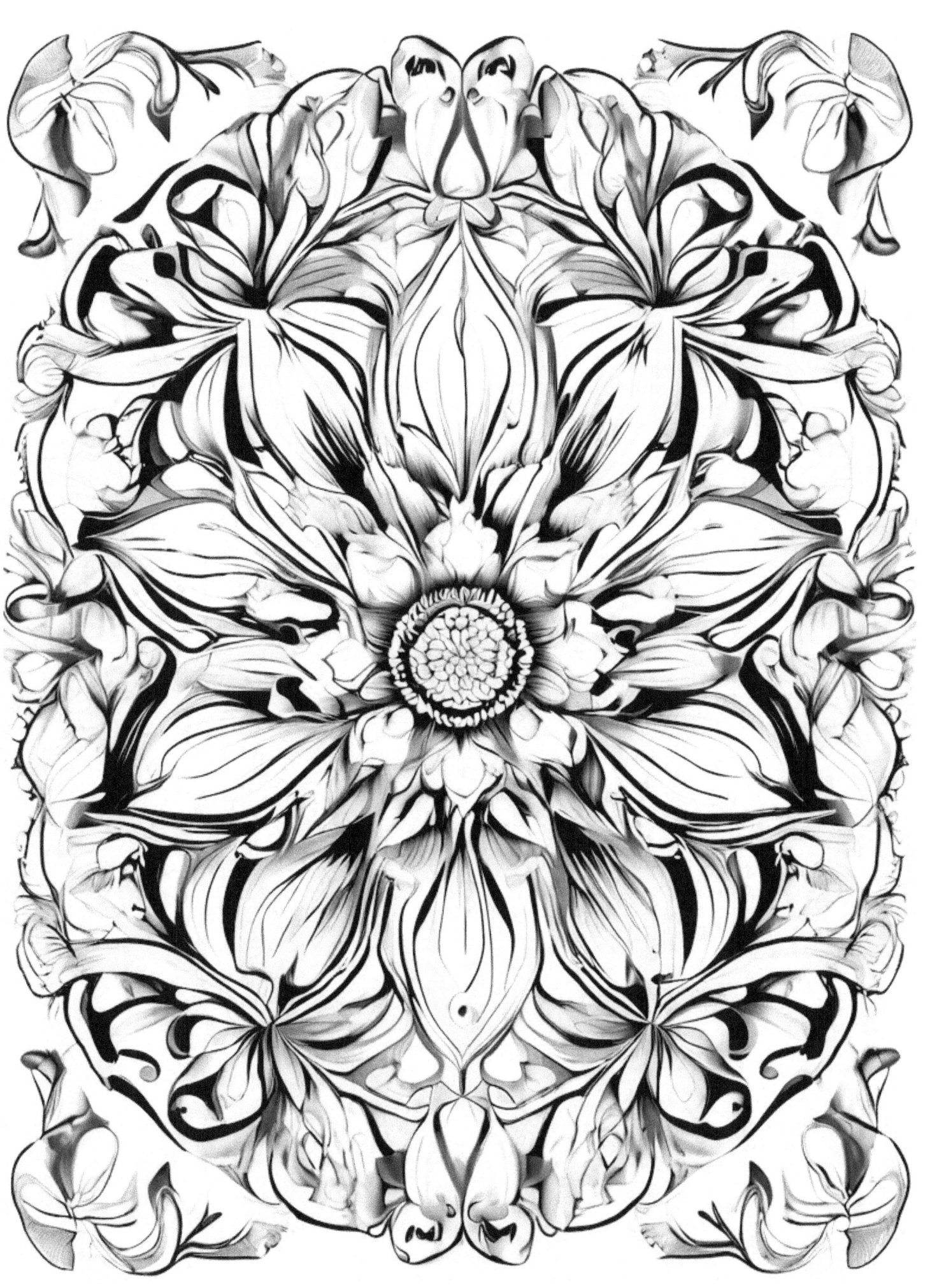

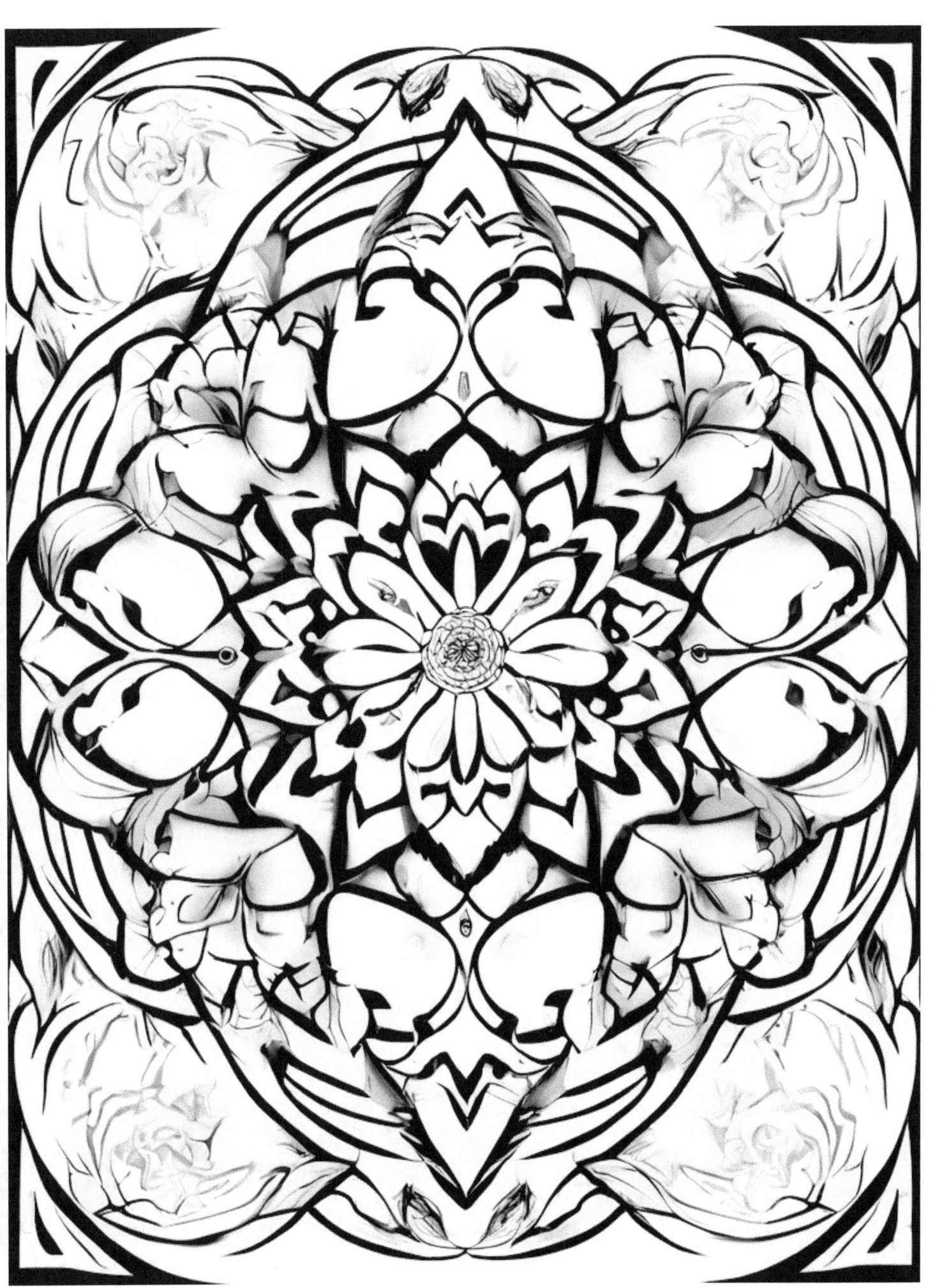

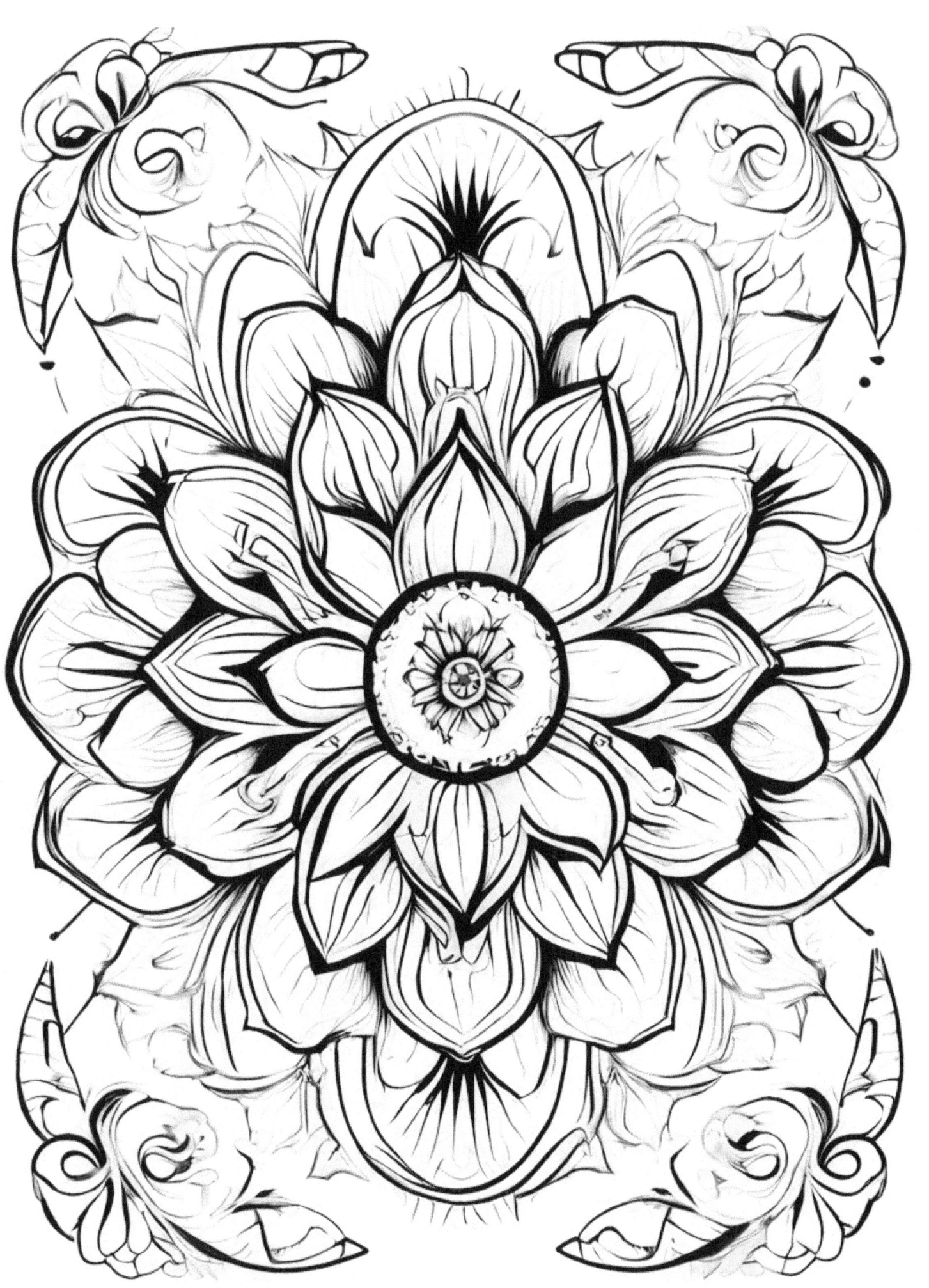

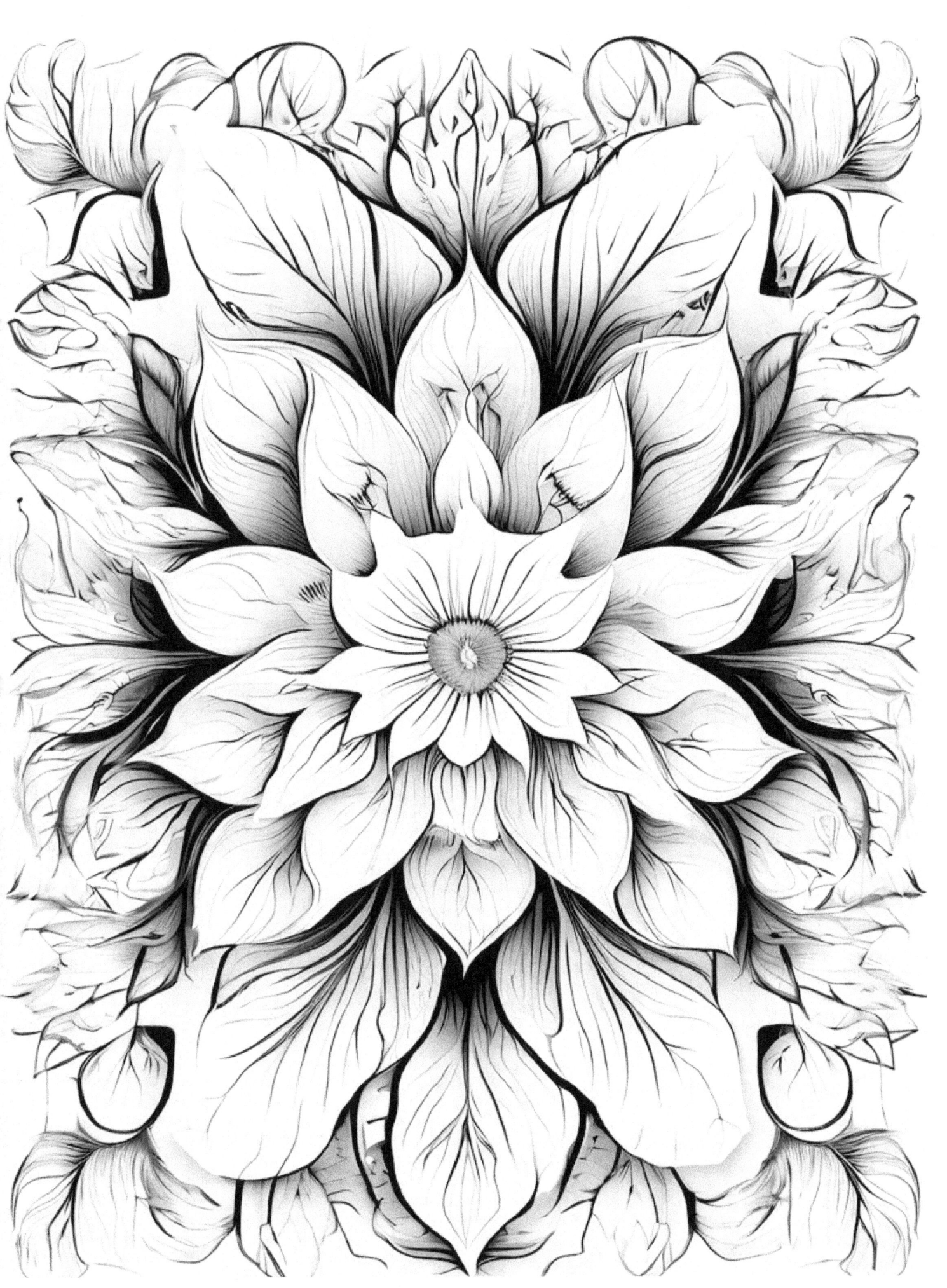

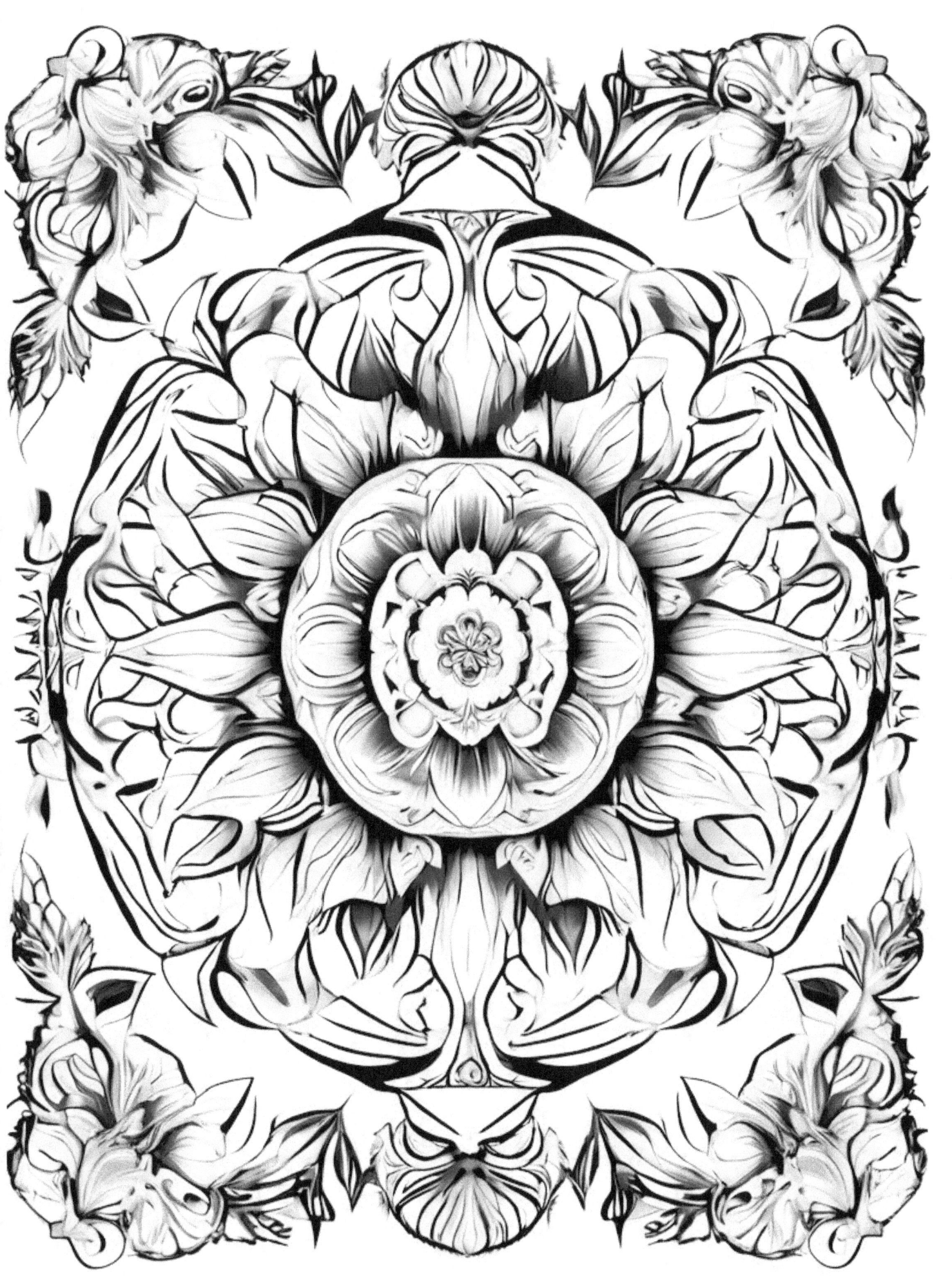

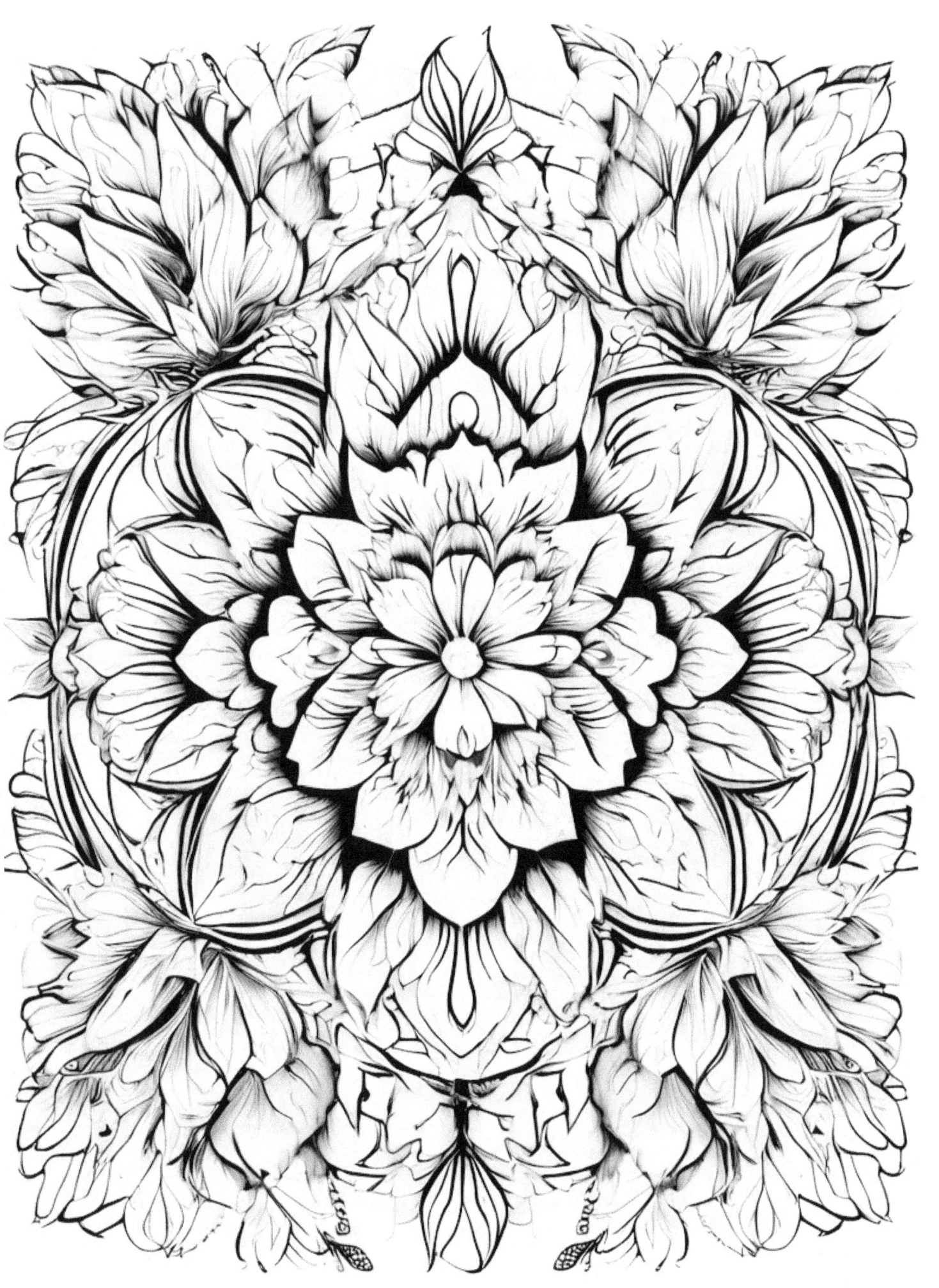

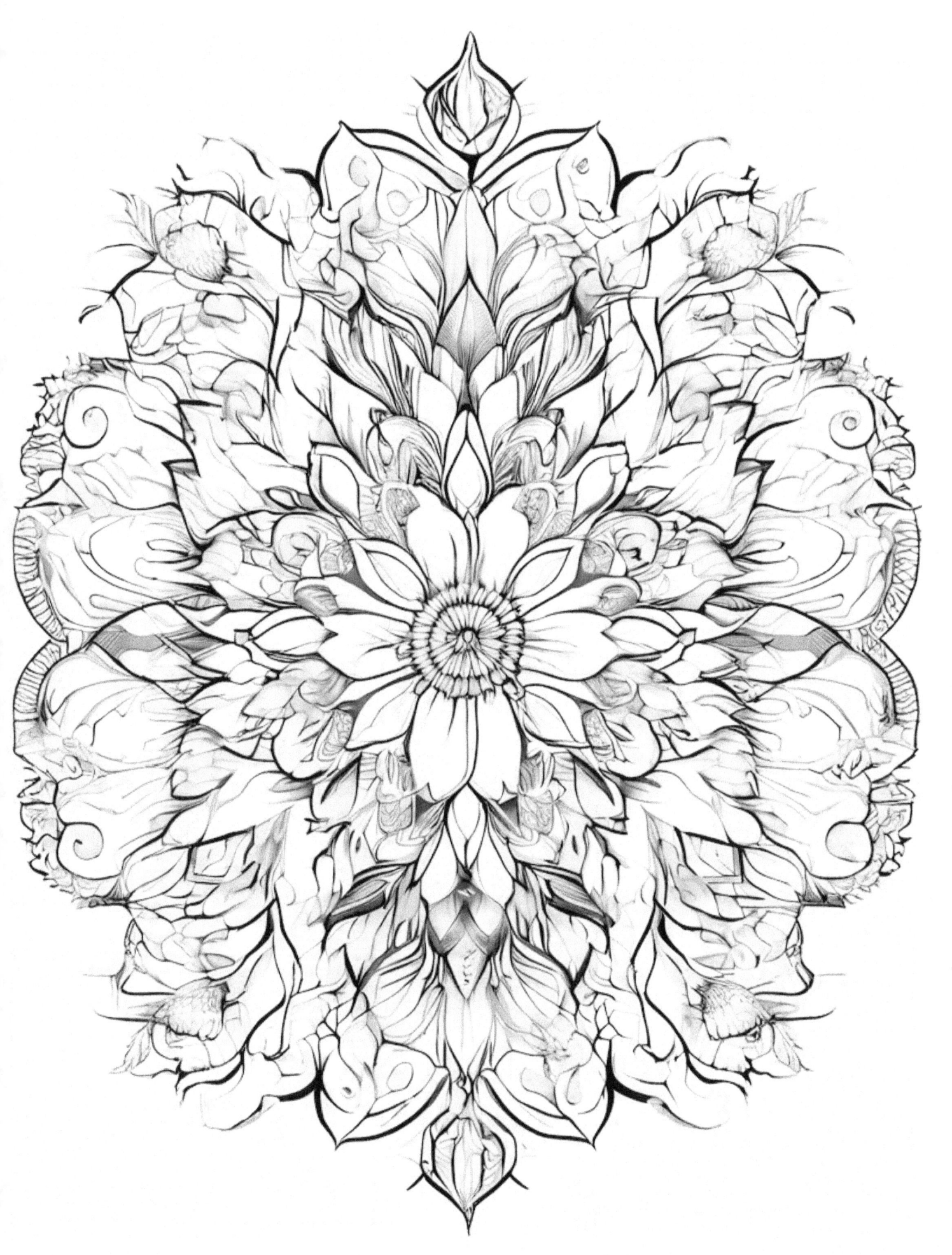

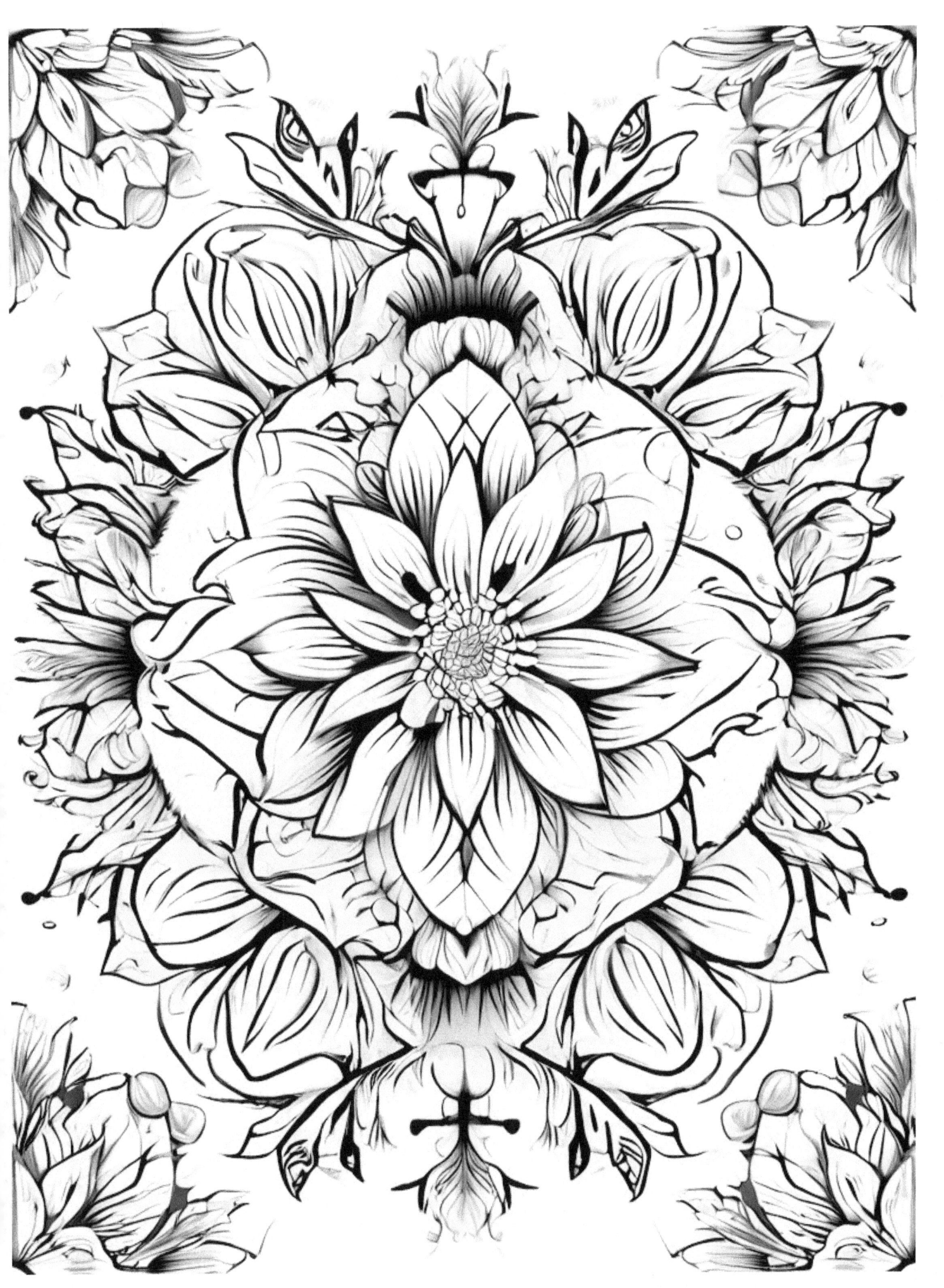

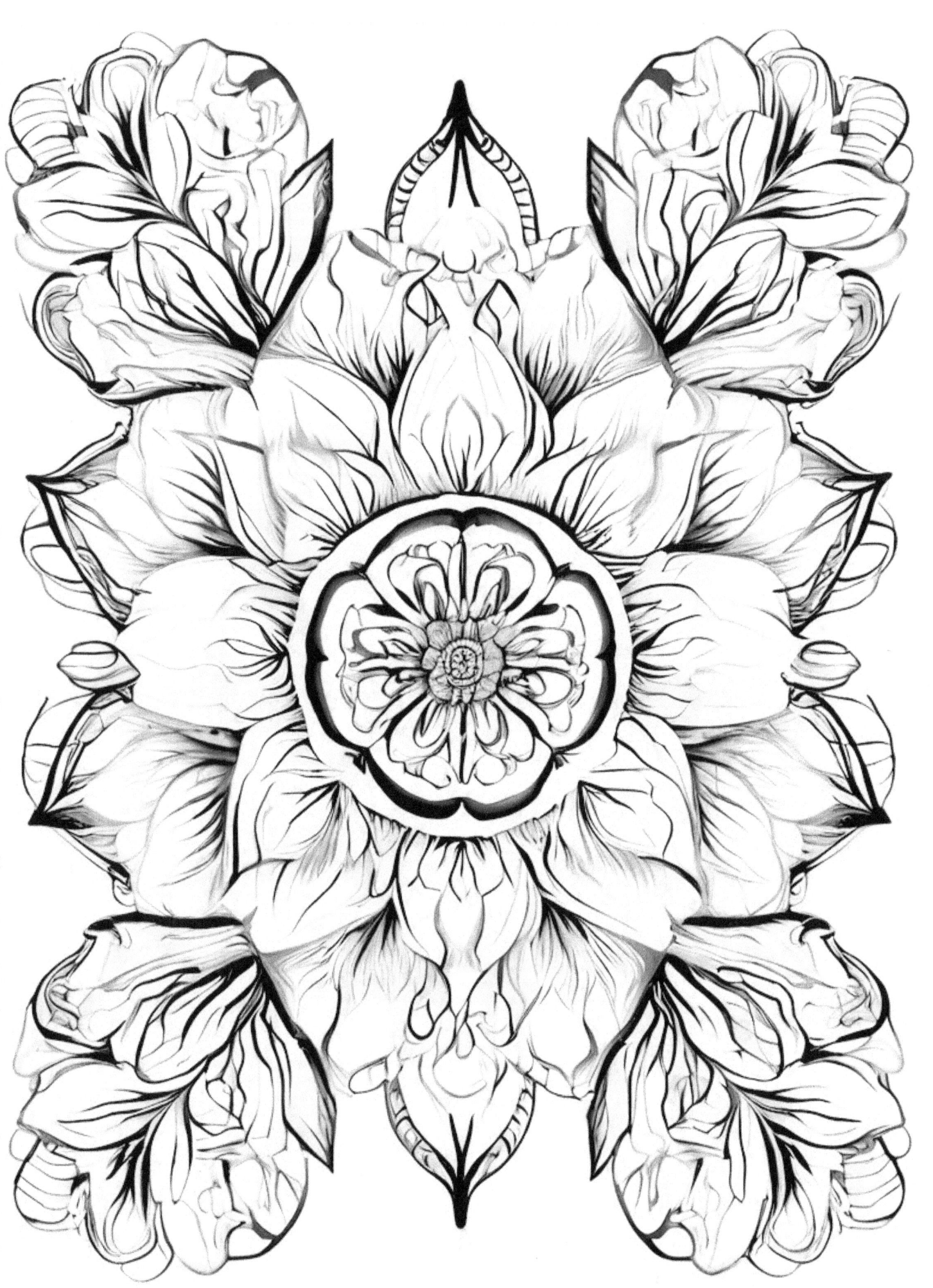

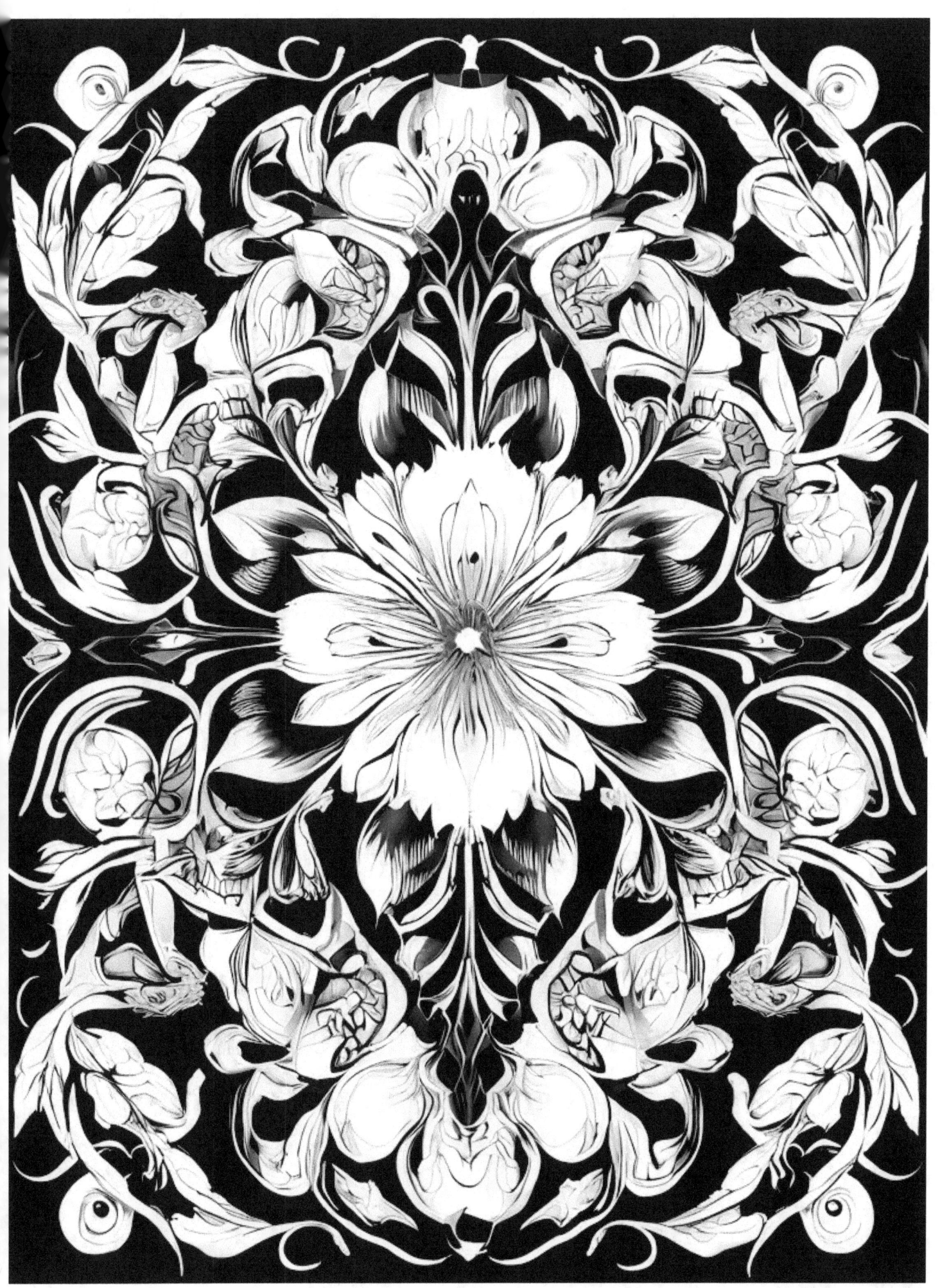

In the pages that are now filled with his colors and inspirations, we witness together the transformation of simple drawings into personal works of art.

As you close this book, carry with you the sense of balance you found among the petals of the mandalas.

May the memories of the hours dedicated to coloring become a thread of tranquility that permeates your daily life.

Thank you for sharing this coloring journey, and may the harmony in petals continue to color the days to come.